the beauty of grace

stories of God's love
from today's most popular writers

Dawn Camp,

EDITOR AND PHOTOGRAPHER

Revell

a division of Baker Publishing Group
Grand Rapids, Michigan

© 2015 by Dawn Camp

Published by Revell
a division of Baker Publishing Group
P.O. Box 6287, Grand Rapids, MI 49516-6287
www.revellbooks.com

Printed in the United States of America

Library of Congress Cataloging-in-Publication Data
The beauty of grace : experiencing God's love right where you are / Dawn Camp, editor and photographer.
    pages cm
  ISBN 978-0-8007-2379-8 (pbk.)
    1. Chritian life—Meditations. I. Camp, Dawn, editor.
  BV4501.3.B427 2015
  242—dc23   2014029692

Published in association with William K. Jensen Literary Agency, 119 Bampton Court, Eugene, Oregon 97404.

In keeping with biblical principles of creation stewardship, Baker Publishing Group advocates the responsible use of our natural resources. As a member of the Green Press Initiative, our company uses recycled paper when possible. The text paper of this book is composed in part of post-consumer waste.

green press INITIATIVE

15   16   17   18   19   20   21   7   6   5   4   3   2   1

For Bryan,
who lets me dream big and believes in me.
You empower me.

contents

foreword

$\mathcal{D}$ear Reader,
      What you hold in your hands or see on your screen right now is an invitation. An opportunity to slow down for a moment, take a deep breath, and know what we all need to understand most: you're loved.

Yes, right where you are this moment. In the middle of your ordinary life, the God who created the universe is whispering to your heart, *I'm right here with you.* That's easy to forget, and what Dawn Camp has compiled for you on the pages that follow will help you remember.

You'll hear stories from women like you—women who have messy lives, hard questions, and busy schedules. They'll tell you how God found them at kitchen sinks and in carpool lines and so many other places they never expected Him to show up. You'll see photos that will remind you of the beauty and grace that can be found all around us if we're only looking.

9

What makes God's love so wondrous is that *He comes to us*. He came to the Garden of Eden to walk with Adam and Eve. He came to a manger to live with us and to the cross to die for us and be resurrected. He's coming again to take us home with Him forever one day. He could have kept His distance. He could have decided we were too messy. He could have said, "Figure out a way to get to where I am." But, no, love always finds a way to get to us and say to our hearts, *I'm here*.

Where do you need God's love to come to you in a new way? It might be in your relationships, or perhaps in your professional life. Maybe in the spiritual desert you find yourself stranded in lately. Wherever that place is for you, you'll find encouragement, comfort, and companionship in these pages. You don't have to feel alone. God is with you and your sisters are too.

I consider Dawn Camp a dear friend, encourager, talented photographer, and brilliant teacher. In other words, she knows how to help people see differently in life-changing ways. And she has created a book that will do exactly that for you.

So let your heart say yes to the invitation Dawn is offering you. With your eyes, your mind, and your heart, enter this space where you're wanted and loved, chosen and cherished, known and held dear. Rest for a while, friend . . . and reclaim the wonder of how much you're loved.

XOXO
Holley Gerth,
bestselling author of *You're Already Amazing*

acknowledgments

To Bryan: you never laugh at my dreams—no matter how crazy—and seem to think I'm capable of anything, like compiling this book. It's amazing to live with that kind of support. You keep me on task when I get distracted and take me to the movies when I need a break. I couldn't do without you.

To my kids: thanks for your patience and willingness to eat fast food while I worked on this book. I love you and our big, crazy life.

To the writers who contributed to this book: I cannot thank you enough for trusting me with your words and your hearts; this book wouldn't exist without you. Some of you are old friends and some of us have never met; you can all consider me a cheerleader. I pray we impact many lives with this work.

To Ruth Samsel, my agent: I'm so glad you're in my corner. Thanks for encouraging and challenging me.

To the Revell family: thank you for believing in me and making my God-sized dream come true. It's been a joy.

To Daddy and Frankie: it does this daddy's girl good to know you're proud of me. Thank you both for your love and support.

To Melissa, Michelle, and Becky: thank you for being here every step of the way, listening to my rambling, and being genuinely excited for me. I treasure your friendship.

To my students, fellow tutors, and parents at our Classical Conversations location: thank you for being face-to-face community for my family, for discussing big ideas, and for the privilege of tutoring your children. I hope I'm modeling classical education for them while progressing through the grammar, dialectic, and rhetoric stages of book publishing.

To the (in)courage gals and DaySpring family: thank you for supporting and loving me and offering honest feedback. This community is the real deal.

To Holley: thank you for believing in me and my God-sized dreams, standing beside me in hard places, and always listening. You're the best Words with Friends buddy a girl could have.

To Jesus: thank You for allowing me to gather the words on these pages together in one place—may it point its readers back to You. Thank You for the life and the family You've given me, for showing me secret places through my camera, and for the beauty of grace.

introduction

My eighteen-year-old son and I sit barstool to barstool, laptop to laptop at the kitchen counter, a twenty-first-century mother/son moment. He's buried in the usual—Avett Brothers videos and guitar tab charts—while I click over to check out a blog post about motherhood that has gone viral.

I'm in tears by the time I finish the first paragraph, laughing hysterically. My son shoots me a look and I shrug and say, "I must need a good laugh," but I think, *I must need a good cry too*. Tears are my default response to intense emotion, often triggered by written words. It's amazing how often the Lord sends me what I need—the right phrase, verse, or story—when I need it.

I don't think it's an accident that Jesus speaks to me through words on a page or on a screen or in a song. John 1:1 tells us, "In the beginning was the Word, and the Word was with God, and the Word was God." Jesus is the Word. If He's a God of words and *He lives in me*, then it's no wonder the works of authors who seek to praise and honor Him resonate with me. Jesus Himself taught with parables: He understands the power of story.

Hebrews 12:2 calls Jesus the *author* and finisher of our faith. Together, He and I pen my story. Even when the plotline isn't clear and I'm playing both protagonist and antagonist, my own worst enemy, I trust Him and He's faithful. Once a week I teach British Literature to a class of tenth graders. I train them to separate characters into two categories: static, those whose personalities don't change and who never learn from mistakes—or dynamic, those who grow in response to the demands and challenges of the narrative.

Without God's grace and guidance, I'd remain a static character in the story of my life.

My mother once told me she worried about me, because for me, there's truth in the saying, "You're only as happy as your least happy child." Life with eight children holds a wide spectrum of joy and sorrow, and a mama feels it all: the thrill of stealing a base, debating for the winning team, or shedding training wheels; the ache of being misunderstood by friends, getting hurt by the boy you never should have trusted in the first place, or dealing with hormones that turn you inside-out and crazy.

I don't know how anyone makes it without faith and God's sweet grace.

In 2 Corinthians 12 Paul asks God to remove the thorn in his flesh, the physical disability that hinders him, and the Lord tells him, "My grace is sufficient for thee: for my strength is made perfect in weakness" (v. 9). Friend, no amount of brawn or bravery will sustain you; in fact, they fool you into trusting in your own power. Accept that you can't do it alone—that you don't even have to try—and rest in the gift of His amazing grace. "For by grace are ye saved through faith; and that not of yourselves: it is the gift of God: Not of works, lest any man should boast" (Eph. 2:8–9).

My Lord strengthens me when I miss my mother, when tears flow so thick I can't breathe, when I don't see the future. He holds me close when my sons grow up and leave, when my daughters think I'm the enemy, when I carry secrets that would break me alone. He loves my children more than I do—how can it be possible!—and I trust Him with their lives, their futures, their souls. He protects us from the unknown and the unimaginable and He rejoices when we rejoice.

While our roles in life are many and varied—wife, daughter, friend, mother, sister, coworker, church member, neighbor— our deepest relationship is with God. If we allow it to suffer, it affects the others. Sometimes He's a father, sometimes an elder brother—and always a Spirit dwelling inside us, guiding. Always we're invisibly connected, bound by heartstrings.

In Revelation 21:5 John says, "And he said unto me, Write: for these words are true and faithful." I like to imagine these words directed to me and all who seek to write truth, such as the stories told in the pages of this book. I pray they remind you of God's love and provision amid the chaos of the everyday; that He cares for you in all circumstances; that no detail is too small and He's numbered the very hairs of your head.

No matter your past or your future, the depth of your sin or the mistakes that you've made, the weariness of your soul or the obstacles in your path, you can experience God's love right here, right now, right where you are.

And that's *the beauty of grace*.

Blessings,
Dawn

purpose

To every thing there is a season,
and a time to every purpose under the heaven.

Ecclesiastes 3:1

a man in a mirror

katie kenny phillips

He stood there, looking in the thrift store mirror. He was trying on a used suit. Out of date. Too big. I couldn't take my eyes off his left hand.

He stood, staring at the reflection. His left hand grabbed at the thrift store tag, keeping it from his mirror view, helping him get a glimpse of what could be. The suit didn't fit. But I think for some reason I knew it had to.

My friend and I were shopping—no real purpose, just perusing deals, but no deals really needed to be found. I recall finding a set of wooden salad bowls and declared right then and there that it would be my first purchase for my new life come graduation. I was moving to California to pursue an invisible thread that pulled at me, and these salad bowls marked the first tangible step in the many that would lead me there. Wooden salad bowls. A quarter apiece.

But this man, this man. He weighed that suit through his eyes and it cost plenty. He stood there for a disconcertingly

19

long time, focused beyond the cloth that hung off his body. Something important was happening between those eyes and that mirror. Something. He held that tag in that left hand as a man might rattle dice before risking it all.

Our frivolity started to feel like an invasion of sacred space and I pulled away from my friend and I watched. I carried my bowls in my arms; he stretched out his to check the length of his sleeves.

We all came into that store for something. I have no idea what invisible thread he was pursuing or grabbing on to at that moment. For me, the bowls were a start of something exciting. An inexpensive gamble, a minor investment. Nothing, really, in the grand scheme of things.

For him, that suit—I couldn't help but think it meant more. The tag, hidden, didn't leave his hand. His eyes, focused, didn't leave the mirror. I wish I had done something important before I left—paid for his suit, left a few bills, something—but such is the clarity of looking backward. I didn't think of it at the time but I knew I was struck down, like a quick flash of lightning, by this man on a random Saturday. I also knew I didn't have any idea why.

My friend and I slowly left the store, me glancing over my shoulder, our simple purchases in bags. We moved on to the rest of our day in a city that beckoned us to be young and fun and carefree. But I quietly tucked the image of that man away, as if he were a secret just for me, a snapshot that would linger awhile.

Why do I still remember that man? Why does he still pull at my heart? Why, if I think of him hiding the thrift store tag in his left hand while studying a suit that would never fit, do tears come to my eyes? Fifteen years later. A man from Milwaukee whom I never knew.

Why? Why? Why not?

We're given these snapshots for a reason, I believe. To learn. To see. To realize that this big world we live in is made up of individual people struggling, trying, growing, living. We are not just a group of anonymous breathing creatures that co-exist together, taking up our fair share of oxygen and soil. We are images of our Creator, beating hearts who love and lose, who buy salad bowls and try on suits. We are people who need jobs, who have failed, who have succeeded, who are trying to turn it around and are trying to point everything to Him.

We need to realize we are images of our Creator. We are meant to love Him and love others. We are meant to live with our eyes open. And it starts with looking at one person at a time. In our homes. In our neighborhoods. In our schools. In our thrift stores in Milwaukee. All this time later that man still holds sacred space in my head. I hope his suit served him well that day and every day after that, for whatever purpose held his gaze in that mirror.

He's one of my snapshots. An image, a blessing.

Beloved, if God so loved us, we ought also to love one another.

1 John 4:11

it's not about me

sara frankl

It's not about me.

That's what has been popping into my head a lot lately when people ask me questions about how I deal with being sick, why I don't get more frustrated, why I don't complain more or why I'm not angry about my situation.

We all want life to be fair. We want goodness to prevail and hard work to mean that life will be easier and . . . that green grass on the other side of the fence that belongs to the people who don't appreciate it? We'd like that to be transplanted into the lawn of the person who spends all day feeding and watering the sparse-looking grass in hopes of a fruitful harvest.

But all of that is "me" thinking . . . and it's not about me.

The plain and simple truth, if we take big lessons in life and strip them down to the bare essentials, is that we are tiny blips on a very big screen. Only God has the capacity to see all of it. He saw all that came before us and sees all that will come after us, and only He can know the role that each of us can play that will best serve Him and each other.

So, my life isn't ideal by our standards. By my standards, it's getting less ideal by the year. That whole living in pain thing? I could do without it. The getting sick thing? Gets old really fast. The never leaving the house thing? I could think of some fun places to go. I miss fresh air. I miss singing at church. I miss dancing until I'm out of breath and riding in a boat so fast if you close your eyes you think you're flying.

But it's not about me. It's about what God can do with my life. I have learned a lot about myself, my faith, my perspective. But that doesn't mean I was given this illness to teach me something. For all I know, God saw this illness was going to be in my body and helped nurture me so that I could use it to affect someone else. And as much as I would like this disease to be gone when I wake up in the morning, if it serves a purpose for another person to see their life or relationship with God in a new light, then I wouldn't ask for it to be taken from me.

Because it's not about me. Nothing about my life is about me . . . it's about who He needs me to be. And how can I complain about that?

Oh, complaining can come so easily for all of us . . . your small house, your flat tire, the promotion that should have been yours, and the grass that grows so fast you don't have the time to mow it.

But what if the small house is so you are next to a neighbor who needs your help when her husband dies? Or your tire went flat when you were driving so it didn't happen when your teenage son was driving and he wouldn't have known what to do? Maybe the promotion would have been a dead end for you and next year a better opportunity will be waiting. And that lawn? Maybe it's the only exercise you do each week and is saving you from a heart attack.

The point is, you don't know. I don't know. But it's not about me. It's about how God can use my life . . . so as far as I'm concerned, even those things that make me want to pull my hair out and scream "Why me?!?" are blessings in disguise. Blessings for me, or for someone else, or for a reason I can't even imagine.

But it doesn't really matter. Because it's not about me.

> Present your bodies a living sacrifice, holy, acceptable unto God.
>
> Romans 12:1

how the boring stuff matters

tsh oxenreider

When I first arrived in Turkey many moons ago to live our family's new life, I was the mother of a two-year-old. A few months later I became pregnant with our second-born. Two years later I became pregnant again and miscarried, then six weeks later got pregnant one last time with our third-born. Most of the years we lived abroad, I was either parenting a toddler, dealing with the effects of pregnancy, nursing a newborn, or some combination of it all.

Of course that's not *why* we moved six thousand miles from our home turf, to change diapers and worship the porcelain god. But that's what I ended up spending quite a bit of my time doing. I'd meet my tutor at a tea house several days a week to learn the language, I'd shop at the local markets, I'd walk to the nearby park to practice language with locals while the kids played, and I'd get to know our neighbors—but otherwise, my life was at home, doing pretty much the same mundane stuff I would have been doing as a new mother in the States.

I found it odd that God brought me all the way to the other side of the world to, well, raise little kids and manage a home.

In fact, I found it more than a little odd. There were many days when I was frustrated at my supposed time-wasting, emotionally exhausted from feeling unused, and quite honestly, a bit bored from it all. At least living everyday life in my own culture meant access to English television and coffee with old friends. What on earth was I doing with my days?

About a year into our life in Turkey, a fellow American friend confided in me, and said, "I've become so frustrated at my lack of usefulness here that I wonder if God brought me all this way not to use me, but for me to better know Him."

Our lives' daily liturgy, when focused on how grandiose or useful or even productive they might be, can become the bastion of frustration when we end our days not having accomplished much more than the humdrum of life. My friend's comment changed my perspective for the remainder of our time abroad because it reminded me that no matter where I am or what roles I've been given, the point of my life is not usefulness but rather knowing God and enjoying Him forever.

This realization is nothing short of revolutionary. Tasks like laundry, nose-wiping, errand-running, and job-clocking stop becoming a burden and start becoming ingredients for our spirituality—a *real* one, where we relish in the fact that we are God's and God is ours, regardless of our usefulness. Even when we're given "big" tasks, like living cross-culturally or serving in leadership, these roles become less of a pressure to perform and more of an assignment to better know

Him when we acknowledge that all of life, big and small, is crammed with heaven.

We are His children, and just as we don't love our own children because of how useful they are to us, neither does God's love for us depend on how productive we are in our days. He is passionately wild about us, even when the majority of our waking hours are spent in the everydayness of it all.

At the end of our life, we won't be able to look back and remember most of the hours of our days, but we'll remember what those hours produced. My hopeful goal is intimacy with God, knowing Him as a true Father and Friend.

> God's definition of what matters is pretty straightforward. He measures our lives by how we love.
>
> Francis Chan, *Crazy Love*

god uses you

jessica turner

A few months ago I had lunch with a new friend. I didn't know her very well, but every time I thought about her I felt prompted to pray. Before this lunch she had shared some struggles going on in her life and her story really weighed on my heart.

We had such a great lunch. She opened up and I was able to speak truth into her life. When I got home, I shared with my husband about our time together, and I said to him, "It was the first time in a very long time I felt like God had used me."

He looked at me and solemnly said, "God uses you in this family every day, baby."

His words meant the world to me. I have been thinking about them for months. And now I bring them to you, because chances are you need to hear the same thing.

God uses you every day.

Do you hear me? When you answer the dozens of calls of "Hey, Mommy?" He uses you. When you get up in the middle of the night to rock your crying daughter, He uses you. When you cook dinner for a group of friends, He uses you. When you are sitting in a cubicle answering emails, He uses you.

Sometimes in life's mundane moments it can be difficult to see that, can't it? But it is true. God created you in His image for such a time as this. And so today, right where you are, I want you to pray and ask God to show you how He is using you. Because if you are like me, you don't think of God using you when you are wiping snotty noses and trying to get dinner done after working all day.

But He is. He uses you every day.

For even the Son of Man did not come to be served, but to serve, and to give His life a ransom for many.

Mark 10:45 NKJV

slow down: to seek

ann voskamp

She loses what's hers and comes plaintive, and I send her looking under chairs, in my library closet, perhaps under our bed? And her mournful cry, like the bay of a hound on the hunt, draws out a brother, and she tugs one end of the couch and he grunts the other. Only a few stray dust bunnies, lost too. She's still hopeful. She digs under cushions, directs her brother to check book baskets by rocking chairs. And when he turns up nothing, she tells him to look behind all the doors.

He's at the back door when it finally occurs to him, to him who has been searching high and low. "What is it that we are looking for anyways?"

I laugh long over carrots, diced and ready to enter a broth already bubbling. Oh my, yes. He comes laughing too, sheepish then knee-slapping. We crack up, notion of searchers seeking but not knowing the sought.

I laugh. Yet isn't it the way that I've lived? Harried and frenzied, haven't I wildly searched only to realize I don't really know what I seek? I just keep running. I just keep racing. I just keep rushing.

When do I slow down, stop, ask: What am I frantically looking for? That would be important to know. Because I can't find until I know what it is I seek. Until I know why it is I race. When I know what I'm looking for, I actually have to go slower to find it. I don't have to keep relentlessly chasing. I actually have to still, to sit.

I know whom I seek. I'll have to slow down, light a lamp, sweep the moments carefully, search attentively, until I see Him. Every moment holds Him, if I slow to see. God's here, Spirit shaping this space. Is there anything else to want?

I turn off all the square, glowing screens. I let the answer machine greet all callers, take their calling cards for later conversation. He's discovered in the quiet.

I focus—try to—even in the whirl of here and children and life. I scratch down a line or two of ordinary. I pluck a note or two from common time, call it poetry. I let music play, light a candle. I try to remember to laugh, to find the humor. I keep a pot of tea on and a Bible open, anchor.

I find a rhythm, a way of seeking, a way of working . . . a way of praying. *Ora et labora.* The laundry, the dishes, the beds, the floors, these have a harmony, a gentle tempo in time. Daily work is not drudgery or pressure-packed, but cadence and beauty. This work is our slow dance with God.

The outer world can drum with its own driving beat, but slow is the rhythm of inner time. Slow is a frame of mind. A soul can always sing slow songs.

Still, too often I glance at the clock, scan the to-do list, and jolt: hurry children, race again, pound the track hard with tasks instead of offering them as a prayer. But I'm discovering: racing means I don't know what I'm looking for. Racing means it's time to remember what my life seeks. He can't be found in the flurry.

Again . . . slow . . .

I give thanks for the gifts to stay present to the presence of God right here.

I sing a hymn. I meditate, turn over Scripture. I make, create, a daughter living like Creator Father.

I slow down this soul to seek Him with my whole heart. The kingdom of heaven belongs to such as these, hearts not hurried by the false construct of time.

She finds what she's looking for and brother cheers. Her mother, Lost Child, slows, seeks carefully, and finds Father.

The angels sing.

> The whole earth is at rest, and is quiet: they break forth into singing.
>
> Isaiah 14:7

soul gardener

stephanie bryant

J feel closer to God, hands in tilled soil, dirt under finger-nails, breeze on my face, sun warm on my back. This is where I came from. Born in a garden. One word away from dirt. My soul knows, peeking into the past, a glimpse into His character. I walk by the vines; grapes will appear soon. Parallels to Red Word stories could easily come to mind.

This morning, I keep walking. My mind on my list of need-tos, have-tos, hoping to be clear soon. Thoughts of the Creation Day creep in. Walking in the cool of the day with Him. What would that be like? Is it like this day?

Growing. The plants are growing. God's mercies in the tender leaves and dark mud.

It all started in the garden. God likes to plant and grow things. Squash. Spinach. Me. His tools look different than mine. As image-bearer, I'm glad to partake. Focused on weed-pulling, a rhythm occurs. Shoulders come down, I start to

breathe for the first time this week. Thought appears—to share this bounty with neighbors. Spinach is ready and more than enough for three households. Making a first pass to clear weeds, I feel proud. Task completed. Harvest time.

I squat, low to the ground. I breathe living air on edible leaves. Near—the only way to harvest fruit. Cupping my hands, I pluck a small crop. Gentle. Prayerful. God be my Soul Gardener.

Then, a large weed—gone unnoticed, camouflaged by the fruit—appears. My eyes had missed this intruder the first pass. My sight isn't always true. The fruit no longer hid the weed. I pause in awe. My life is the same. Holy Spirit–produced fruit in me but not perfection yet. Weeding, pruning, and fruit harvesting—never one without the others. No more choking out growth; I extract the intruder. Revelation to my mind.

Jesus says,

> I am the true grapevine, and my Father is the Gardener. . . he prunes the branches that do bear fruit so they will produce even more. You have already been pruned and purified by the message I have given you. Remain in me, and I will remain in you. . . . Those who remain in me, and I in them, will produce much fruit. For apart from me you can do nothing. . . . When you produce much fruit, you are my true disciples. This brings great glory to my Father.
>
> John 15:1–8 NLT

God is close, my Soul Gardener, pruning and weeding, especially when I'm producing fruit.

> Ye shall know them by their fruits.
> Matthew 7:16

the big picture

For my thoughts are not your thoughts, neither are your ways my ways, saith the Lord.

For as the heavens are higher than the earth, so are my ways higher than your ways, and my thoughts than your thoughts.

Isaiah 55:8–9

overcome

dawn camp

I stare at a pair of old-time portraits my parents made years ago and, looking down, realize I've dressed in one of my mom's shirts today. It's started again, unconsciously, this yearly counting down to the day in mid-March that marks the date when she gave birth to me, her first child, and also passed from this world seven years ago.

A friend calls, needs to talk, to process her recent birth experience, and I am back in the room where I delivered my seventh child, just six months before my mother's death, when she held my new baby in the middle of the night and I hemorrhaged, unseen (we never told her). I relive the eighth birth, the culmination of nine months of confusion and wonder that my body didn't understand what my mind assumed: that surely there would be no more children with her gone. *Lord, why did you give me eight children and take my mother?* I'd questioned. Later that child would be the saving of me at a time I when desperately needed a mother's presence.

I look in the mirror and I see my father's eyes, my mother's and grandfather's cheekbones, my grandmother's chin. I see another grandmother's hands that remember family recipes, an aunt who could also lose herself in words on a page, another who embodied silent strength. And I feel loss, deep and overwhelming. Loss of these influences that molded me, all gone save one. And then I see Him.

In that moment I am overcome—no longer by what I've lost, but by what I possess. I cannot outlive Him. I cannot outlove Him. He will never leave nor forsake me.

And it's enough. It will always be enough.

> Leave me not, neither forsake me, O God of my
> salvation.
>
> Psalm 27:9

on comparing yourself

arianne segerman

*E*very login, every click-through, nearly every email has the potential to make me feel so inadequate. The beautiful homes on Pinterest shine a light on my crayon-scribbled, fingerprinted walls and the many piles of laundry waiting to be folded. The bloggers with their gorgeous photography point out how badly I need a lesson on how to use a camera. The beauty tutorials on YouTube make me wonder how I ever survived not knowing how to apply liquid eyeliner before now.

Every new success on Facebook reminds me of my failures. It's so very easy to get sucked in, isn't it? But oh, sister, Jesus wants us to be reminded of truth. To ignore those lies that we aren't enough. To step away if it becomes too much.

We all, each of us, are in different seasons of life. We make different choices and God has different plans. Jealousy can so quietly slip in and take root, and slide its vine-shaped lies around our throat and squeeze. Squeeze until we're nearly suffocated and can't even hear God's Spirit wooing us back to Him.

The best weapon against this stuff? Gratitude, quiet (unplugging), prayer—and more prayer.

What to pray for? Ask God to refine your heart and buff out those harder edges toward others that need softening, the edges that make you feel like you don't measure up. The edges that make you forget how blessed you really are, even if those blessings don't look like everyone else's. It's grace to realize, when these issues pop up, that we can rest in the truth: Jesus is in the business of redeeming. And it's grace when He forgives us for forgetting it.

God doesn't require us to succeed, he only requires that you try.

Mother Teresa (attributed)

it happened on a tuesday

kayla aimee

It was on a Tuesday, the eighty-fifth day, that I walked through the glass doors to hear the alarm flashing, to see the doctors and nurses working frantically over her limp, gray body. Lifted up and carried out, flailing against the arms of the strangers removing me from the scene, I didn't realize I was screaming until they gently told me to stop.

It was on a Tuesday that I discovered the whole of my relationship with the Lord could be condensed down to a thin, flat red line pulsing across a small black screen. *For God so loved the world that He gave His only begotten Son. . . .*

Nine months prior I had stared down at a positive pregnancy test and whispered an age-old prayer of thanks. I was Hannah, grieved in my infertility and rejoicing at the long-awaited promise of a child.

You count your pregnancy by weeks and I was at twenty-five when the doctor laid her hand on my shoulder. "We're taking the baby," she said. I breathed deep of the oxygen mask, gripping the cold hospital bedrail and the place where not seeing becomes believing as they cut my daughter from me. Everything changed.

And in that moment the once-indefinable weight of glory was spelled out across the scale they laid her bare on. One pound, eight point six ounces. One hundred and fixty-six days in the neonatal intensive care unit.

People often ask me how my faith was tested during that time. "Not tested," I answer. "Stripped."

I had thought myself knowledgeable. As former vice president of the FCA, answers were what I had. I studied the Bible. I knew stuff. And around my heart I amassed a collection of religious tokens that began to cast a shadow over the genuinely important. In my most desolate of moments everything else I had wrapped around my faith fell away and left exposed the single most defining truth: God is who He says He is.

In a fit of incompatible emotions I both raged at Him and begged Him to heal my daughter here on this earth. Either way I would be forever changed, marked by this shift where my faith became intangible. That was where I was that Tuesday, with my face pressed against the glass, suspended between hope and desperation and clinging to the same answer regardless of the outcome: *Jesus is Lord.*

Scarlette purses her lips when she is concentrating on something; her brow furrows as she gingerly flips the cardboard page of a rhyming book. "God loves you more than the deepest sea," I read to her.

She is curious about my tears, tracing the path they've made down my cheek with her finger. "Mommy is crying because she's happy," I tell her. She's not even two so I can't explain to her that these simple rhyming words in her favorite book are just a portion of the mercies that are new every morning.   45

One day I'll give her a bigger book with a soft leather cover and tell her it's a love story.

The truth is, I did nothing. I didn't live well or believe well or stay strong in my faith. I laid with my face on the floor in the darkness and just let the small, inextinguishable flame of truth do what it is meant to do. No one will write my name in history books as a woman of great faith nor will I pen studies giving guidance on overcoming adversity. They'll simply reference an ancient text and see where in one life, it was true:

For where I am weak, He is strong.

> And he said unto me, My grace is sufficient for thee: for my strength is made perfect in weakness. Most gladly therefore will I rather glory in my infirmities, that the power of Christ may rest upon me.
>
> 2 Corinthians 12:9

when god says "stop," he doesn't always mean "quit"

rachel anne ridge

*H*ave you ever come to a roadblock in your ministry or job and wondered why God would lead you along so clearly only to bring you to a sudden standstill? That's happened to me many times as I've followed His leading and then gotten confused when I felt Him say *stop*.

Wait a second, Lord. I thought you said we were going from A to Z, and we're only on M! Is this where I'm supposed to quit and move on to something else? This makes no sense!

Recently, when I came to a stop sign that's in an odd place along the country road near my house, I was reminded of those confusing moments in life. That sign seems to make no sense either. It is placed on the road where a smaller lane "Ts" into it—a lane that is seldom used, and has its own stop sign for drivers to give way to the larger road. For about ten years, we drove through that tiny intersection without a stop sign there, and without any incident to warrant one being installed.

And then one day, there it was. A big, red stop sign with flags and a blinking light atop it to alert drivers to its new placement. I personally ran that stop sign about twenty-five times out of sheer habit. And each time I'd curse its meaningless existence. There was never any intersecting traffic and it was such an annoyance! (Insert angry muttering here.)

Finally, it occurred to me that the stop sign was not really intended to protect drivers at that intersection. No, it was actually to get drivers to bring their cars to a halt so they would proceed with caution through the *next* stretch of road.

You see, right after the stop sign is a dangerous curve that leads to a bridge. Every month there is at least one new accident at that spot, caused by speeding drivers who can't make the sharp turn in time. By the time they reach the curve they can't slow down fast enough to avoid taking out the rails. I can't count how many times I've seen tow trucks hauling wrecked cars away from that location.

At first the city tried reflective stripes on the guardrails, but there were still too many accidents. Then they installed blinking yellow lights around the curve. No improvement. Then they tried a yellow caution sign with a squiggly arrow. Cars continued to plunge though the barrier.

Finally, someone must have had an idea. "If we put a stop sign *well ahead of the danger*, drivers will come to a halt, assess the situation, and proceed with caution around the curve."

Brilliant. Accidents at the curve have been greatly reduced simply because *coming to a stop ahead of time makes drivers aware of what's around and ahead of them.*

Maybe you're at a personal "stop sign" and are wondering why God has placed it in your life when He has clearly shown you the direction He wants you to go. Instead of quitting or pouting or throwing a fit, perhaps you should consider that His purpose may simply be for you to stop long enough to gather wisdom, get the lay of the land, look around, and move forward slowly. He knows that the path ahead gets tricky, and by briefly arresting your speed, He is giving you a chance to get your bearings . . . and trust His leading. Sometimes it takes a "stop" to get us to pay attention.

Look. Listen. Take note of what's ahead . . . and proceed with caution.

> We can make our plans,
> but the LORD determines our steps.
> Proverbs 16:9 NLT

i bet you think this song is about you

mary carver

I have a rash on my face. An awful, red, itchy rash. All over my face, my neck, my chest and, as of this morning, my hands.

The medical explanation is an allergic reaction, possibly to poison ivy blowing around the park on a windy day. The treatment is a long list of prescriptions, sticky ointments, and hand washing until my knuckles crack. But none of that really matters.

A few days ago, my husband and I had time for a quick dinner alone before he headed to work. On the way to our new favorite Mexican restaurant, I combed my hair and reapplied my makeup. By the time we arrived I felt kinda-sorta pretty. But the first thing my husband said when we sat down in a corner booth was, "What's wrong with your face?"

Now, he truly asked out of concern, and had no idea that I'd been imagining he was noticing my good hair day as we sat eating salty chips. And he was right to be concerned. As I carefully touched my chin, I realized that spot I'd been mindlessly scratching earlier in the day was now flaky and bumpy and, yes, itching like crazy again.

As the night wore on, the rash spread over my jawline and up over my cheek. And by the time I woke up the next morning, my face was nearly covered with red, bumpy blemishes that were screaming to be scratched.

A not-so-quick visit to urgent care resulted in an inconveniently located shot, prescriptions, and instructions not to touch the infected parts of my face. The doctor assured me that I was not contagious and should just enjoy myself at my daughter's birthday party that afternoon.

Easier said than done! As my family began arriving for the party, it wasn't the itching or the inflammation that bothered me so much. It was the humiliation of showing others my face—my red, bumpy, ugly face. I wished for a shirt that said, "Yes, I have a rash on my face. No, it is not contagious." I longed for a mask or a veil or a shroud of any kind to cover myself. And I wanted to just hide in my room (and scratch) until everyone left.

Several days after the party, my face was still a wreck. My mom encouraged me to look on the bright side and be thankful I didn't have to go to an office looking like this. She's completely right, but I still felt like a leper, avoiding eye contact and walking on the opposite side of the grocery store aisle.

Simply put, I felt ugly. I'd tried joking my way around my feelings and acknowledging what a ridiculous situation this was, and remembering that it was temporary and not the end of the world. But what nailed me in the chest every time I left the house or caught a glimpse of myself in the mirror was this: I. Feel. Ugly.

Today, as I was wondering about the surprising strength of this reaction, I realized it stems from vanity and misplaced self-value. Immediately, Carly Simon began belting "You're So Vain" in my head, taunting me and echoing those catchy words. The song might be stuck in my head for several hours now, but I'm thankful for the reminder that focusing on my appearance, my face, my beauty (or lack thereof) is never going to make me happy, rash or not.

I turn to the Word and am reminded that God sees our true, inner beauty—and that is really all that matters. No rash, no gray hairs, no wrinkles, no chubby or too-skinny parts can take away what He sees when He looks at His creation, His beloved.

Perhaps today your own face is blemished, your jeans feel too tight, or your hair won't lie flat. Take comfort in these words of truth and remember that you are beautiful in God's eyes.

- The LORD does not look at the things people look at. People look at the outward appearance, but the LORD looks at the heart (1 Sam. 16:7 NIV).
- So we do not lose heart. Though our outer self is wasting away, our inner self is being renewed day by day (2 Cor. 4:16 ESV).
- Charm is deceptive, and beauty is fleeting; but a woman who fears the LORD is to be praised (Prov. 31:30 NIV).

· Your beauty should not come from outward adornment, such as elaborate hairstyles and the wearing of gold jewelry or fine clothes. Rather, it should be that of your inner self, the unfading beauty of a gentle and quiet spirit, which is of great worth in God's sight (1 Pet. 3:3–4 NIV).

when giving up
is the right thing to do

kristen strong

On a sunny Saturday my daughter Faith and I attend a gymnastics competition, and we marvel long and applaud loud as Faith's best friend, Cora, soars with beauty and grace in every event. She is exquisite, I tell you, especially on the balance beam. Indeed, the beam is her microphone; she grabs it with confidence and positively *sings*.

As I survey the room and all its amazing athletes, I can't help but feel our presence at this gym—the same gym where Faith took gymnastics herself—is bittersweet.

It was the previous fall when the last of the aspen leaves dropped from their golden glory that our girl dropped on a mat in a gymnastics exercise that left her head throbbing and her sobbing, scared over being "numb and tingly." The exercise didn't look frightening; she didn't fall awkwardly or in any way that made me jump out of my chair. But we don't mess around with numb and tingly. So after the ER trip, X-rays, and a CT scan, we discover that the critical bone—the odontoid—that protects her spinal cord is malformed. This bone protrudes from the second vertebrae and the malformation means part of her spine is not as protected as it should be. Without this extra protection, any jarring of the neck can cause numbness. Or worse, much worse.

This leaves us numb and jarred into a new reality, but for no one more so than our Faith. Gymnastics is permanently removed from her world while neurosurgeons are added. Surgery is performed and after months of limited mobility and wearing a neck brace, Faith is able to resume many of her normal activities. However, gymnastics isn't one of them.

Losing gymnastics is a hard thing for our active girl to accept, this saying goodbye to a love and a dream of hers. So given the fact that Faith hasn't been to this gym since the day we discovered her broken neck and she said goodbye to gymnastics herself, I worried about how she would react. Faith was never at competition level, but she had dreams of competing and the loss of that was a true lesson in the hard faith.

Watching her friend, Faith cheers long and loud without an ounce of envy or bitterness. She grins, laughs, and waves to Cora when she catches her eye. More than once I tear up proud, because y'all, unless you've lived under our roof for the past year, it's hard to appreciate all this. We head home several hours later, and no sooner do we walk through our front door than her tears come, the wishing things were different while mourning the loss again.

We all grieve on our own timetable. And sometimes in the grieving we place dreams on altars, our own Isaacs we sacrifice. I wish this could be a one-time event, but more often it's a daily offering. Whether with a weak smile or a healthy dose of tears, we wake up and give up again and again.

Like He did with Isaac, sometimes God puts a holy stop on the sacrifice. Other times we are called to let go and give up our plans for good. But when we are able to turn those hands upward to God and then move them together in celebration for others, we give a sacrifice of praise.

Holy sacrifices are never in vain. We take the hard faith one day at a time, walking blind to the future but holding on to the One who sees every single day.

A little later, Faith's tears dry. With excitement in her voice, she tells her brothers how beautifully her friend competed. And I smile, thankful to hear the heavens sing as a whole new kind of beauty and grace soar right on up to the sky.

> He healeth the broken in heart, and bindeth up their wounds.
>
> Psalm 147:3

on living a good story

laura parker

There's been a lot of talk about living a Good Story the past few years, and sometimes I wonder if my husband, Matt, and I have lived the dramatic story for the wrong reasons. When I walk away from inspiring movies I'm left with a question: Does a heroine spend the two hours of the movie *pursuing the most gloriously dramatic film*, or does *a gloriously dramatic film just naturally tumble out of her pursuit of more important things*—like love, redemption, victory, the cure for cancer, that kind of thing?

Shouldn't a Good Story be the *result*, not the *motivator*, of an epic life, a faith worth remembering?

I feel like Matt and I have gone with gusto after the wild, epic kind of life (or what we understood that to mean in our youthful, take-the-world-by-storm twenties). We read John Eldredge's *Wild at Heart* after college and we were all about pursuing a career that filled our hearts and a journey that pushed the envelope of "safe." We sold everything and moved to Saipan, an island in the Pacific with palm trees and dirt roads, and then did it again to do ministry in New Zealand, with its wild places where the epic Lord of the Rings trilogy was actually filmed. We've also thrown ourselves into four businesses over the last ten years that took great risk—and have all failed. Matt's led trips overseas and done edgy things that would make your grandmother nervous in an effort to connect with teenagers. We've packed up babies and our life and moved halfway around the globe . . . for the sake of the girl in some dark room somewhere, for following where we believed God to be leading . . . maybe,

maybe, in part (should I admit it?) for the sake of a more Dramatic Story.

And I think I am learning that this final motivation isn't really a right or pure one.

I had several people tell me, during our most recent visit to the States, "You are doing something *so* important. And it just makes my life feel so behind, so *normal*."

And the older I get, the more I realize that maybe the true heroes, the ones *really* living out brilliant stories, are the ones who never make much of a headline, anyway.

It's the ex-wife who forgives her cheating ex-husband, even if he doesn't ask for it. It's the daughter who takes her Alzheimer's-afflicted mother to doctor's appointments and McDonald's every week. It's the husband who works a job he *doesn't* like, for the sake of the family he loves like crazy. It's the man who leaves a hugely ridiculous tip for the waitress, because he sees she has to be eight months pregnant and there's no ring on her finger.

One of the greatest lies we can believe about our life is that if it doesn't have the setting and the scenes of a summer blockbuster then it's not really that valuable, seeped in God-reality, or the stuff of epic goodness. And that has to be a lie, right?

Because Mary didn't *set out* to be Jesus's mother. And Peter was *just* fishing with his buddies. And I can't see Gandhi or Mother Teresa clawing for the spotlight at any point. Those dramatic stories just naturally *played out*; I'm not so sure they were sought out, from the opening scenes, when the boat first shoved off the dock.

Maybe it's me. Maybe I'm the one splitting hairs that don't really matter all that much anyway, but as I sit and think about my own story and the living of it, I wonder if I haven't gotten a little too caught up in a quest for drama. I wonder if I haven't followed my own idea of a Good Story, *assuming* that a Good Story has to be Hollywood, on par with *Braveheart* or *The Last of the Mohicans* or *Titanic*.

Because while it's true that no one wants to order popcorn and watch a two-hour depiction of a single mom working two jobs, checking her kid's homework, forgiving the guy who abused her, slipping an extra ten into the offering plate, and cleaning toilets on a Saturday morning, maybe *that* life has more of the makings of a Good Story than we realize.

Or embrace.

> I had always felt life first as a story: and if there is a story there is a story-teller.
>
> G. K. Chesterton, *Orthodoxy*

surrender

Humble yourselves in the sight of the Lord, and he shall lift you up.

James 4:10

when you want to give up

holley gerth

There will be moments when you've had enough and it's all too much. When you feel that way . . . *give up*.

Yes, ma'am. You heard me right. Stand and raise your hands as high as you can. Then turn your open palms toward heaven and tell God you're done. You're handing it all over to Him. *Giving up*. Then ask Him what He wants to give you in return. Take hold of what He offers with both hands and bring it back to your heart.

Strong girl, I know it's hard for you to think that way. You feel like you need to prove you can handle all this. You worry that you'll let someone down. You're afraid of feeling weak or out of control. But sometimes the bravest thing you can do isn't to just keep going. Sometimes the most courageous act is surrender. Sometimes true strength is knowing when to *give up*.

So find a quiet spot as soon as you finish reading this, ok? Somewhere you can raise your arms up high and let the tears stream down if you need to. Say what you need to say to God, then open your hands and your heart.

It's time, friend.

> Hear, O LORD, when I cry with my voice: have mercy also upon me, and answer me.
>
> Psalm 27:7

on losing place

amber haines

I begrudge my little dog at 5:00 a.m. because she needs a walk and it feels like I just went to bed an hour ago. Most of the time my husband, Seth, takes her, but this morning I woke at a lovely 3:45, too excited to drink coffee perhaps, so here I am in my pajamas in the middle of the night where I can hear the leaves touch, whispers of autumn.

The canopy above our house is thick, so it's easy to feel huddled in the dark, but when I walk beyond our yard with my end of the leash, I stand in a gasp at the sky, just as clear and wide open as can be. It took light years for these stars to reach my view. My mind's morning routine is, first thing, the Lord's Prayer, and I've learned to stretch that thing way out; all I can do this morning is

Hallowed, Hallowed, Hallowed.

The breeze edges on cold, and my legs are bare. I am exposed, aware of Eden within, God with me.

Inside, the coffee drips, and it's an old house so it smells a little like a granny kitchen with my basil cleaners and wall plug-ins floating on top. I love the way the blanket lays on the couch, how the throw pillow is catawampus, and even the basket full of papers feels right. Backpacks in a row under the window, the little dog-food bowls, all my books and dishes displayed on open shelves: we couldn't have made up anything better than this when we were looking for a house.

We're finding our groove for the first time in maybe a year and a half. Now that we have it, I tense up like I have reins in my hands. I told Seth again, last night: I don't want to move from here. I hope we never have to pack. It's funny because our rental agreement lasts for eleven more months, and what goofball starts worrying that far in advance?

The stars tell me what I already know. Kingdom comes. And it is big. And I have a part to play, or I wouldn't be here. Sometimes I wonder if I really trust God or not, what with how I grip the reins. I worry that I won't trust Him when the time comes. But I know whom I have believed, and I am convinced that He is able to guard until that Day what has been entrusted to me: my short time, the gifts, all the many kids. I have believed, and He will guard. That's the deal, I suppose.

I like to look at things up close, how my son Isaac likes to take a rock and note its divots and swirls. I think of telescope the same as a microscope, and I imagine what I am, as if there's a petri dish here in the Milky Way. I am a speck, and even that hardly describes how small. How do I get to be a part?

I imagine the perspective, way out at the very edge where Voyager 1 has taken its thirty-six-year journey into the magnetic highway. It's now at the cusp of our solar system. How spectacular to be eyes at the end of that scope. Years before now, it turned back around for a single snapshot of the earth, a tiny blue dot, a speck of a pixel in a great brown streak, less than a fish-tank rock in the ocean.

The God of human life, and of light and space, matter and time, I wonder of Him, that He made dew and sex and secret species of orchids. His DNA is code on my heart. Why? These are the things that make people stare crazy holes into walls.

But then my son Titus walks in with his daddy's eyes, his wavy hair, a saggy morning diaper, and the biggest smile, and he runs to me and pulls a blanket into our chests. Everything was serious, but then the morning laughs. We snuggle tight. His nose touches mine, and there a kiss.

I feel for a fact that we are small and precious things in God's sight. His very children. I won't be afraid to lose my place. I may as well not. Kingdom come.

> When I consider thy heavens, the work of thy fingers,
>   the moon and the stars, which thou hast ordained;
> What is man, that thou art mindful of him?
>   Psalm 8:3–4

peace in the pieces

eighteen days in december

kelley j. leigh

I open my refrigerator and a large jar of strawberry jam falls to the floor with a heavy thud and splat like an ostrich egg dropped on a sidewalk. My fridge is smashed full to capacity with food from generous friends who unload meals, offer condolences, and slip away.

Eighteen days ago my family set up and took down a wedding. We welcomed visiting family and hugged them as they left. We quickly put up makeshift Christmas decorations, and before we could take down the stockings we found ourselves preparing for my mother-in-law's funeral. The linear span of days on my December calendar has felt more like a dumped puzzle than a plan.

I stare at the red jam as if at a bloody crime scene on my kitchen floor, a messy crisis of sharp glass and sweetness.

Yesterday, my husband and I drove from a cremation meeting to a recovery room. A couple of days ago, I held the clammy hand of my husband's mother and whispered to her like a midwife. She breathed her last rattling breath and ended a lifelong fight with disease. Several days before *that*, my musician son broke his guitar-playing hand in a sledding accident. The injury required intricate surgery.

So we rode in a post-concussive stupor from funeral home to hospital. We traveled between death and healing, all in one day.

Our best-laid plans are just pine needles on last year's fresh-cut Christmas tree. We can enter a kitchen in the morning and expect fresh coffee and dishes in the dishwasher. We can look at the orderly wall calendar with tidy scheduled events and suppose all will go as planned. And this may go on with an accompanying sense of false certainty for months or even years on end. But at some point, refrigerators drop food like unexpected bombs. Days deliver injury and departures unplanned.

Christmas sat down like a heavy iron anchor in the middle of our eighteen days. Silent Night candles raised by hands in a dark church on Christmas Eve reminded me about "*Son of God, love's pure light*." A room full of voices lifted flames of hope and by some gift of grace I remembered. No matter how dark the world becomes, no matter how broken, there is always redeeming grace, always available light and peace.

Over the last year, my tall, philosophical husband, Steve, and I have been learning a new way of doing life. We are 69 learning the practice of Peace—the kind with a capital P. I used to think I was in charge of maintaining my own version of peace through planning, through control, through avoiding failure and striving to make everything ok for everybody. Life events, no matter how joyous, were stressful. My life was about managing circumstances and avoiding disruption. So I used to spend a lot of time in the bathroom hyperventilating or crying before donning my Superwoman cape. I utilized a lot of ways to self-medicate and soldier on in order to make life look and feel as close to perfect as possible. In the end, it was all a very false kind of peace that made me sick emotionally, physically, and spiritually.

But everything is different now.

Yes, I still stress. I get sidelined. On certain days I am tempted to grab my Superwoman cape. But now I am more able to be present and feel, in sickness and in health, in joy and sorrow. I am learning to see unexpected circumstances and disruptions as my portal to God instead of my personal battles to win. I am in a clumsy learning curve of turning to my Divine Anchor when the storm kicks up. It feels clunky and unnatural most of the time, but together my husband and I are in a process of learning healing prayer and relationship with God.

I am learning how to run to God instead of the bathroom. Why? Because we nearly drove our marriage into a ditch trying to be God on our own. Turns out, peace is possible in the middle of chaotic seasons, but only if I am *not* the peace source. For me, God is. Jesus has to be.

I use a rag and dustpan to swipe the first pass over my jam and glass mess. I squint and strain to see tiny splinters of sharpness scattered where feet will walk. Trash lid opens, sticky shards and sweet berries lump and fall together into the garbage.

We can plan sacred weddings, not the breaks that come with marriage. We can attempt to arrange for the end of life, never the date of a last breath. We can strive to be the self-sufficient savior, but in the end that strategy will never work. Certain mysteries dangle out of our reach by design. There is only one true Peace.

"And he will be called Wonderful Counselor, Mighty God, Everlasting Father, Prince of Peace" (Isa. 9:6 NIV).

On my knees, I wipe up the remnants of chaos and see the reality of our eighteen days. I see a sweetness and mess divinely mixed of brokenness and healing; of bright unexpected stars and angels in the sky; of eternal vows, final breaths, and infinite freedom.

On our knees, we find Peace in the pieces.

For God is not the author of confusion, but of peace.

1 Corinthians 14:33

if you could ask god for anything

christin ditchfield

*J*f you could ask God anything—anything at all—what would it be? If you knew He would answer, tell you anything you wanted to know, what would you ask?

I can think of all kinds of questions—fun questions and frivolous questions, curious questions and "just because I'd like to know" questions. But I probably wouldn't ask any of those, at least not this side of eternity. They can wait.

The questions that I really want answers to are a lot more serious, more personal, more pressing. The "What should I do?" kind . . .

Where is my life going? Which way should I take? What should I do? What is Your plan or purpose for me, for my friends and family, our church, our community, our country? This situation or circumstance? What's going to happen in the future? How is this all going to work out?

And the "Why?" kind . . .

Why did You? Why didn't You? Why do You? Why don't You? Why won't You?

And the "Where?" kind . . .

Where were You? Where are You?

Last summer I hosted a virtual "Vacation Bible School" for women on my blog. We were reading through the Gospel of John together. In John 12:16, we found a kind of explanatory note that appears often in the Gospels: "At first his disciples did not understand all this. Only after Jesus was glorified did they realize" (NIV).

Only after.

So many times, Jesus told them directly who He was, not just in parables or with metaphors. So many times He told them exactly, in no uncertain terms, what was going to happen to Him—His death on the cross, His resurrection. And they didn't get it. They didn't understand.

I have to wonder. What makes me think that if He answered all my questions today—if He told me everything I wanted to know—I would do better than the original disciples? They lived with Him day-in and day-out for three years. Face-to-face. They saw Him with their own eyes. They heard Him with their own ears. No guessing whether or not that was His voice!

But somehow they couldn't wrap their heads around what He was telling them. They had their own preconceived ideas, their own limited perspectives, their own thoughts and feelings that prevented them from seeing and hearing Him clearly.

The truth is that sometimes we aren't really hearing. We aren't really listening. Because we don't want an answer. We don't care what the answer is. We're not asking—we're protesting, registering our objections or our complaints.

Even when we are earnestly, truly, desperately seeking Him, His answers can be hard to come by and hard to grasp. Not that we don't ever get them. Very often we do. God, in His mercy, does reveal things to us all the time. He promises to give us wisdom whenever we ask for it (James 1:5). His Spirit constantly guides us and leads us. Daily He teaches us to know Him and trust Him.

But especially when it comes to those "Why?" questions . . . I'm not sure there's any answer that we could fully appreciate, any answer we could completely comprehend, any answer that would bring us any real closure or comfort on this side of eternity.

Despite how we feel about it right now, the answer might not change everything. It might not change anything.

It's not wrong to ask questions. All through the Scriptures God tells us to ask. We can learn a lot about Him and about ourselves just by asking. Being honest about what we think and how we feel. But when we don't get any answers or don't get the answers we want—the answers that make sense to us—we have to remember what Job learned after he had questioned God and God had questioned him:

> Surely I spoke of things I did not understand,
> things too wonderful for me to know.
>
> Job 42:3 NIV

He is God. And we are not. The day may come when we do get answers—when we do understand. But until then, Jesus has promised us something far better than the answers we seek. He has promised us peace. His peace. Perfect peace.

He is all the answer we need.

> For my thoughts are not your thoughts, neither are your ways my ways, saith the LORD.
>
> Isaiah 55:8

choosing here

joy forney

As we haul bags into a stuffy taxi to make our way to the airport, he leans over toward my frowning face with a smile and says, "*You know, I think maybe going on vacation isn't good for you. It's too hard for you to go back.*" He's right. As I mentally prepare myself for the "going back" it is always hard. I sip my last decaf venti iced nonfat vanilla latte (say that fast!) that I ordered *in English* as I think over my life.

I've always known what I would be leaving, moving overseas. I knew the first time, the time when we filled the big yellow bags to the brim and smiled in front of them, full of energy and excitement as we said goodbye to family, friends, and the life we knew. We were off to begin our adventure, the excitement of new things, the allure of the unknown.

But now, six years later, I know what I am choosing to come back *to*. I know how the dog yelps nonstop day after day after day, crowding out my sleep, wearing me down like Chinese water torture. I know the feeling of sweat dripping constantly down that spot where my cleavage would be if I *had* cleavage. I know that sinking feeling when the electricity goes off again, and it's anybody's guess as to when it might come back on. I know the smell of the garbage piles on the side of the road, the ickiness of full sewers, and the constant noise of a city too packed onto its tiny island frame. I know.

And yes, there are the moments where I dream of pulling a Wonder Woman dive out of the taxi and crawling back under the fresh white duvet cover with the remote and watching *Cake Boss* until I fall asleep.

But then. Then I remember the *why*. This life is short, and I want to live it surrendered, not comfortable.

Jennie Allen, in her book *Anything*, says, "*If we believe that this life is temporary, that belief alone changes how we live it.*" I want this temporary life to be one that I can't live on my own, one that I need His strength for each and every day. Living in this way brings joy deep down in my soul. My sweet Jesus gave it all for me on the cross. He loves me so intently and He has given me the chance to offer back to Him a life of sacrifice.

And the truth is my life, the messy one, where I have to rely on Him to get me through, is more beautiful than any sea view, any candlelit dinner, or any afternoon spent journaling at Starbucks. The messy life I have, the one He chose for me, is far more beautiful than any comfortable relaxing moment I can imagine, because He is in it.

And now, knowing exactly what I am in for, I choose it all again.

> Offer the sacrifices of righteousness, and put your trust in the LORD.
>
> Psalm 4:5

when all you have is a half-empty basket

kristen welch

I don't have much to give. But I have a lot to do.

Do you know that place? The one where you have a list a mile long, pressure that is suffocating, responsibility that is frightening, and a host of people asking for more?

Sure you do. If you're a mom, this is what you call life.

Yesterday someone asked me to email them a link and I burst into tears. Apparently I found my breaking point and it all came crashing down with a recipe. A RECIPE, people.

My house is a pile of suitcases and lists and stressed-out people. There have been ugly words this week, tears over lost things, and grief over things we need to lose. We are the most unlikely crew to get on a plane several times a year and fly across the globe to Kenya and spend time serving the girls and babies of Mercy House, the nonprofit organization our family started in 2010 to provide hope and opportunity for pregnant teens living in extreme poverty.

We don't always know where our *yes* will lead us. And we don't always feel qualified to follow. But we go.

I can't help but think of a little boy in a Bible story from a long time ago. The one who said *yes, I have a lunch to share* in a mass of hungry people. His basket was half-empty or half-full, depending on how you see baskets. He didn't have much. His small offering wasn't enough to meet the need. *Sounds familiar.*

Jesus didn't need the contents of that basket. He just needed the little boy to offer it.

And today, with stacks of laundry teetering dangerously, arguing children, a sink full of dishes, and loads of packing and decisions before me, I'm holding up my basket too. It isn't much, y'all. My offering looks a lot like a couple of stale pieces of bread and leftover fish. *Hardly worth giving.*

But I'm holding up my half-empty basket to God. It's filled with a desire to tell a story and a lot of fear and it's all I've got. The world says it's not enough to feed the masses; they say I'm not enough. And they are right.

But God is enough. He is strong where I am weak.

When God breaks my offering, He breaks me. I want to give my life away. Piece by piece. He blesses it. Multiplies my insignificant gift and makes it enough.

And maybe today you need a cup of coffee and a long break. A break from your half-empty life, your not-good-enough offering. Your smallness. Your list that is too long, your messy house, your marriage that is half of what you want it to be, your bills that are too big, your calling that is too hard.

Listen, close. This is God's truth whispered in your ear: God doesn't want you to be a perfect mother or wife. He isn't waiting for you to get your act together. He isn't shaking His head at your pathetic basket offering. He simply wants you to offer what you have.

Because He will make it enough.

> Then he took the five loaves and the two fishes, and looking up to heaven, he blessed them, and brake, and gave to the disciples to set before the multitude. And they did eat, and were all filled.
>
> Luke 9:16–17

why you don't have to do all the work

holley gerth

I spent years as a striver. I knew what it felt like to live with a full schedule, a pounding heart, and not enough sleep. I thought if I didn't try so hard then I would let someone down . . . God, people I loved, myself. I clung to my goals and ambition like a lifeline.

Then slowly, gently, God began to pry my fingers open. *You don't have to hang on so tight*, He seemed to say. What happened next came as a complete surprise. *I began to see that by doing all the work I hadn't left any room for God to work on my behalf.*

Opportunities popped up out of nowhere. Relationships developed. Words flowed.

And even better . . . when people asked how it happened I could truly say, "*God did it.*"

I do believe that we're called to be faithful stewards with what we're given. But I was going far beyond that. I'd become a spiritual workaholic. And God wanted to teach me about a little thing called grace. I still don't fully understand it. I probably never will this side of eternity. But I know this . . .

I've traded exhaustion for joy. Striving for more peace. Anxiety for laughing a whole lot more than before.

Sure, I still have stressed-out days. But those are an exception . . . not a lifestyle. I don't ever want to go back. I ask God to help me not to, because I know my own heart well. I'm sharing this with you because, friend, maybe you feel like you have to do all the work too. Let me lean in and whisper to your heart, *"Loosen your grip, enjoy your life, love on the people right in front of you."*

Open hands can best receive what God has to give. Open hands can best be raised to praise Him for what He's doing in our lives.

Open hands let people focus not on the calluses from our hard work but on the nail-scarred hands of the only One who truly deserves the glory.

He arose from before the altar of the LORD, from kneeling on his knees with his hands spread up to heaven.

1 Kings 8:54

my poverty (and yours)

edie wadsworth

This week we are swimming in abundance.

I spent the weekend making all manner of preparations. While Stevie smoked back ribs all day yesterday, the rest of us flew into a frenzy of buying and storing and cleaning and prepping and sewing and ciphering. All this to make sure twenty-eight people knew how thankful we were to have them in our lives.

Everywhere I turn in my house, there's excess. I have bowls and stemware and linens and food and candles and silver galore. There is wealth and bounty aplenty.

Everywhere, that is, except in me. It's the poverty of my own heart that scares me to death. It's my inability to be who I was created to be. It's my impatience and unkindness to my children—the lack of grace and love and joy. It's the tally of hurts done against me that I keep record of and file away for later use.

It's the wretched cycle of my own sin that makes me sick.

And when I stood at the end of this week, looking at the trail of brokenness, that's when I saw the *beautiful paradox of want*. This poverty of spirit that plagues me is the beginning of repentance. This is where I find God. When I have come to the end of my resources, to the last shred of hope in myself, that's where He waits. And the truth is, the sooner we discover this poverty—that we all happen to share—the sooner we can learn to live from *His* wealth.

Because everything is God's.

And if our hands weren't so full of our own decaying riches, He'd show us what abundance really looks like. It looks something like *peace, joy, love, kindness, gentleness, goodness, faithfulness, meekness, temperance,* and *forgiveness*.

We may be the richest (most indebted) country on earth, but we live in sheer destitution.

Our lives look more like strife, sadness, cruelty, harshness, wickedness, faithlessness, stubbornness, excess, and blame. At least mine does, if I'm honest.

And I hate my inadequacy. I want, for all the world, to be capable and industrious—to have it all figured out, to have the perfectly coiffed life. And you probably do too. We don't want to feel our need, our desperation.

So we hide, we medicate, we pretend, we run, we seek cheap relief wherever it may be found. But at the end of that long, scary road of our stubborn self-sufficiency and our rusty heap of riches and our swirling addictions, God waits. Because He is gentle and kind and faithful and full of peace and forgiveness.

He is love incarnate. And He became flesh to know this very pain. He took on this desperate poverty in which we live to give us wealth untold. He is our Father. And our inheritance cannot be measured.

And if we are wise, we will learn to thank God for those things that remind us of our true condition: the very circumstances that break our hearts and cause us to despair.

Those are His gifts to us, to help us see clearly.

By nature, we hate the heartache that drives us to Him and keeps us begging for relief, begging for answers, begging for the scraps from His table. But from that lack, God will give us heaven. Let us not forget that it was in desperation that David wrote Psalm 51 and from prison that Paul wrote Ephesians and Colossians. It's in our poverty, not our abundance, that He will give us His kingdom.

We don't have to *try* to be poor in spirit to receive His kingdom. *We are poor in spirit*, and we must beg Him to show us our emptiness in order that He may fill us with the bounty from His table.

Everything is His. And so everything is yours.

Oh, taste and see that the LORD is good!
Blessed is the man who takes refuge in him!
Psalm 34:8 ESV

trust

And they that know thy name will put their trust
in thee:
for thou, LORD, hast not forsaken them that
seek thee.

Psalm 9:10

the kind of faith
that changes your life

emily p. freeman

I stare out the morning window; the outline of my tired head stares back at me, wispy hair out of place, wild. The sun isn't up yet, only the faintest faded line of pink lingers over the trees out back. *This slow rising happens every morning*, I think to myself. As I wrap my hands around my warm cup, I can't help but rush ahead into the day. Even though the house is quiet, I'm running on the inside as if things are in full swing. My feet haven't moved but my soul is rumbling.

Mercifully, the Lord whispers His presence with me and I'm pulled back to this minute. I consider how God called the light *day* and the dark *night*, how He spoke the days into being *just one at a time*. He still does it that way, evening and morning and evening again. And the days roll into one another in a watercolor line of elation and planning and laughter and frustration. Sometimes it feels like my life is a gray arrow right through the center, pushing ahead to get on with the next thing, desperately wishing I could see far off ahead.

It isn't usually the big things that cause the most trouble and doubt. With the big things, it is so obvious I'm out of control—the diagnosis, the job insecurity, the safety and well-being of my family. Instead it's those everyday things that are covered with my fingerprints. I try to get things I already have, things like acceptance, worth, security, love. Maybe everything we do is to get one of those needs met. Finish the list—*I am important.* Apologize for my messy house when the neighbor comes over—*I need your acceptance.* Don't let them see my weakness—*I need your approval.*

We are terrified of the mystery. We want our manager hats to remain firmly on our heads, skirts smoothed, shoes shined, plans lined up in neat rows. At the least, the suggestion that we are not in control is laughable. At the worst, it is offensive. I have a degree, you know.

And so I stand there next to the window, pink sky lightening with each moment, and consider the invisible place in me where my spirit and God's mingle together. I used to think that a mature faith would bring with it clear pictures, that as I walked with God I would see life big, wide, and spacious. But that is not what is happening, and if that is what you expect it can feel like perhaps your faith is shrinking. Because instead of being lifted up on a cloud to see the big picture, instead of tilting back my head and laughing at those silly things I used to worry about, I am shrinking down into a small place, a place where I can barely see two feet in front of me, much less into next week.

Everything in me wants to fight the unveiling of the anxieties that threaten to overwhelm, push them back from showing up in my day. Christians aren't supposed to be anxious, right? I want to ignore the smoky unknown; it is counterintuitive to let the anxieties rise to the surface.

But we must let them rise up so that we can release them into His hands. Speak the fear out loud so that He can give words of truth. Don't run away from those places where it seems your faith is small. Run into them, look around, be honest about how it feels as you stand there. And know we have a God who can handle it.

I put my cup on the table, breathe in deep the air of a new day, pray without words to a God who knows. I become aware of His acceptance of me, and not because I finished everything on my list. Truth can be a slow rising, making no difference at first. But as each moment weaves itself into the next, as we believe Him in the great right now, His truth becomes a strand woven into the fabric of our minutes. This moment-living is sweet. This moment-living reminds me of who is in control and who is not. This smallness is to be celebrated, not despised. I dare not trust myself with the next step. A mature faith says *I am desperately in need of a source outside of myself.* I always have been, but now I know it.

We can do no great things, only small things with great love.

Mother Teresa (attributed)

let him create the masterpiece

lisa whittle

I am ever capable of stifling the work of God in my life. My children—they remind me of this, again, as often they are my teachers.

I watched them last night as I allowed them unedited and free rein in the kitchen, to make *whatever they wanted, with certain ingredients* in a fun, Food Network-esque cooking competition.

And when it was over, beautiful things lay on the plates . . . from the food, their hands, their minds that had been allowed to be creative.

I wondered, silently, as they showed off their masterpieces, why it is that I let my own preferences, plans, structures stifle such important moments. *I don't want a mess in my kitchen. I need things in order. I have a plan for the night and this does not fit into my schedule.*

And I lament because I know . . . I have surely missed many masterpieces along the way by not allowing creative hearts to interrupt my plans. And I'm grateful that for once I got it right: I took my hands off and let things happen. I am reminded, again, of how I often get in my own way.

I get in God's way too. A product of the *get it done, figure it out, work out a way, stick to a schedule, pull it together* culture . . . I stifle the creative work of God in my life because I don't want things to be messy, out of my control, or not within my plans. (Even though I know that rich history with God and experiencing His power in my life *produces more faith*.) The truth is, friends, when we stifle our Creator we cheat ourselves. Because anything we are able to produce will never measure up to what He can do.

But what if we decided not to settle for the things our hands can do? What if we chose to give the reins to God and told Him *for real* to take us down roads we don't know and promise only to stay with us?

What if we forgo our plans, stop worrying about the mess, and let the Creator be as creative as He wants to be with our life? *I suspect we will see beautiful things.*

Because the Master is always capable of a masterpiece.

For we are God's masterpiece. He has created us anew in Christ Jesus, so we can do the good things he planned for us long ago.

Ephesians 2:10 NLT

when life spirals out of control

margaret feinberg

$\mathcal{M}$y four-pound superpup, Hershey, brings me so much joy. Even with his small size, he certainly packs a powerful punch in the ways God uses him in my life.

I think back to a few years ago, when Leif and I met him for the first time. Tiny. Timid. Fearful. As we gently picked him up to take him home for the first time, fear filled his body. We were taking him from everything he knew and was familiar with—and it showed.

No eye contact. Tail between the legs. His tiny body trembling. The whole drive we tried to offer comfort. We stroked his soft fur. We held him close. We kept repeating: *Trust us. You're going to be okay. Just trust us, little Hershey. We're going to take care of you.*

But he didn't listen or understand. Like a horse with blinders on, he was only focused on the fear right in front of him,

not realizing that we had his best intentions in mind and a full life to offer him.

A God-thought filled my head. *You do this too.*

I recognized God's gentle whisper. In the midst of change, I too fidget in fear. I try to hold tight to anything familiar.

Blinded by fear, I am only focused on what could go wrong. I quake in my boots when all along God is whispering to me, *Trust Me. I've got this all under control. Don't be afraid, My beloved. Don't worry, My child. Just trust.*

Like Hershey, I find myself in situations where the ground is taken out from under me. Life begins to spiral out of control. I swing my arms frantically as I try to find anything to hold on to. When all along God is whispering, *Trust Me. I've got this.*

Not just the adversity I'm facing, but whatever adversity you're facing too—He's got this.

> Whenever I am afraid,
> I will trust in You.
> Psalm 56:3 NKJV

navigating the unknown

lisa leonard

Our oldest son David, who is seven years old, was born with a disability including missing fingers on his left hand, small size, delays in all developmental areas, and a heart defect. Whenever I explain David's special needs to someone, I'm always quick to tell them how amazing he is—how his personality lights up a room and everyone who knows him is blessed by his sweet nature.

We recently found out David would need surgery and that the surgeon would need to open his chest to repair the hole in his heart. And since we got that news, I've been sort of a mess. I'm not someone who usually struggles with fear, but the thought of David's chest being opened makes my knees wobble and my throat tighten up. It's hard to think about, let alone talk about, with actual words.

I don't like feeling afraid, and I find myself broken before the Lord. Navigating the unknown makes me realize how out of control I am. It also reminds me that God is in control. The world is not a random, chaotic place but rather every moment of every day is overseen by a capable, loving God. *Who knows me and knows David.*

And He loves us. This is where my hope lies. This is how I navigate the unknown.

> Why, my soul, are you downcast?
>> Why so disturbed within me?
> Put your hope in God,
>> for I will yet praise him,
>> my Savior and my God.
>>> Psalm 42:5 NIV

the god of the storm

dawn camp

Weather, like life, is changeable and unpredictable: two-and-a-half-mile-wide tornadoes. Flooding. Wildfires. Severe thunderstorms.

Two weeks ago a storm hit Atlanta, the kind where family calls to make sure you're ok when it's over. It caught a friend between the grocery store and her car, with winds so fierce she couldn't open the car door, puddles in the bottoms of her bags, clothes soaked through to the skin.

One of our AC units quit and I didn't want to heat up the house by using the oven, so I was on my way out the door to get pizza when the sky bottomed out. One look at it changed my mind.

Sometimes circumstances smack us like a flash flood, no warning, unexpected. I want to cross my arms over my head and seek cover, but no umbrella can protect us from a life storm. Employers don't care. Children disappoint. Friends

are absent. Even the best husband goes to work and leaves you alone. What's a girl to do?

Trust Jesus. He's constant, He's capable, and as incomprehensible as it seems, He cares.

> When I consider thy heavens, the work of thy fingers,
>   the moon and the stars, which thou hast ordained;
> What is man, that thou art mindful of him? and the
>   son of man, that thou visitest him?
>
> Psalm 8:3–4

When the storm ended, the kids called me outside to see the clouds: God's stunning fingerwork in the sky.

It's easy to become overwhelmed. Some days I can hardly put one foot in front of the other. Maybe you feel it too. But listen: God is in control, even in the storm. The clouds are the dust of His feet. The storms show us we're not in charge, we're in over our heads; we have days when we say *I did not choose this path*.

When trust is all that's left.

The LORD hath his way in the whirlwind and in the storm, and the clouds are the dust of his feet.

Nahum 1:3

cow skipping

mary demuth

Sometimes God gifts us tiny, reflective gifts . . . little *cadeaux* that thrill our hearts and paint pictures in our minds we don't soon forget. Running along an open field, I spied a cow (or actually she spied me). She looked up at me, startled, as if I were an anomaly on this road. Maybe I was. Clad in all black running gear with the sun behind me chasing my shadow. I smiled at the mama cow; she chewed her cud in a happy sort of way.

A few feet later, a passel of calves looked up. A small flock of blackish birds twirled around one calf, nearly crowning her with wings. She leaped. And leaped again. If she were a colt, I'd say she bucked. In that moment, God reminded me that He had penned words about skipping calves.

I ran home, happy to have made myself run again, and I found these words:

But for you who respect my name, the sun of vindication will rise with healing wings, and you will skip about like calves released from the stall.

Malachi 4:2 NET

Of all the talk these days (from the Lord to me and from His servants to me) about rest, this verse cemented it all. I feel like I've been in a stall the past several years, in a holy holding pattern that consisted of hay, straw, grain, and longing. I've seen the pasture. I've longed for it. But the stall has kept me bound.

I'm thankful for the stall. There I've learned humility and dependence upon the One who provides the grain. I've learned to trust. I've learned the fine art of grieving. Even so, I realize there are seasons in this life. Wildernesses, even. Could it be that God is opening the latch to the stall door and pushing me out into the great unknown? Beyond the wilderness?

I am a calf, sometimes barn sour, wanting to grovel in the muck of my own safe world, but God beckons me beyond to green pastures, frolicking birds, nurturing mothers. He wants me to find safe pasture, to learn the art of resting beside quiet waters, to not be so self-conscious that I can't dare to skip in the daylight.

Oh dear, dear, dear Jesus. Help me to skip today, to revel in rest and freedom and joy and newness of life. Release me. Help me to be willing to be released. Free me indeed. Set a garland of birds above my head like a crown of dancing praise. I want to be free from the grief that's haunted me for far too long.

The LORD is my shepherd; I shall not want.
He maketh me to lie down in green pastures: he
leadeth me beside the still waters.
He restoreth my soul: he leadeth me in the paths of
righteousness for his name's sake.

Psalm 23:1–3

fill that glass half-full

the golden rules of fearless living

bonnie gray

The other day, someone asked me whether I was a *glass-half-full* or a *glass-half-empty* type of person. I hadn't been asked that in a while, and stopped to think about it.

I used to totally see the glass half-full when I was younger. Until I got burned living that way. Then I became the glass-half-empty type. I started seeing how everything could go wrong, to protect myself against making mistakes.

The funny thing is, life did seem to get better. I felt more in control. I took pride in successfully predicting how the chips would fall. But I noticed a side effect of such "smart" living. I started losing my edge. *My faith edge.*

I started disappearing in a shroud of avoiding rejection—whether it was relational or taking risks with new things. Changes were subtle, but my consistent picks to stay safe yielded a life of predictability . . . creating a wall of people-pleasing and fearful calculations that made spontaneity and joy pretty scarce.

Thank God, my memories of the glass-half-full life came back to bug me every so often. In the form of . . . regrets.

I hid myself from the possibility of pain so well, I reached a point where *the pain of regret outgrew the pain of rejection.* I got it wrong.

I will be burned regardless of how I see the water in my glass. Rejection is a universal human experience. The difference in living a fearless life versus a fearful life, however, is unmistakable. *One seeks out the good, while the other lives to control the bad.*

The Four Golden Rules

Will I live creating a trail of regrets of what I could have, would have, should have done? Or will I choose to live, *trying* to be fearless, and actually do this thing called life? I came up with the Four Golden Rules of Fearless Living and started coming out of my shell:

1. Choose the *harder* choice.
2. *Keep it real* with others.
3. *Practice* seeing the glass half-full.
4. Pray for *courage* to make mistakes.

These four pointers challenged me to keep my faith edges sharp. Each time we attempt one of the above, we are exercising faith. We risk rejection for the opportunity to live true to the desires God's placed in us. We exercise choice, trusting that God's plan for us is bigger than our mistakes.

It's ultimately a question of whether we trust in God's goodness. Will He:

Catch me *when I fall?*
Replenish friends *if I'm betrayed?*
Heal my broken bones *if I'm hurt?*
Restock the storehouses *if I'm robbed?*
Still bless me, *when I make mistakes?*

I'm not saying it's easy—but man, consider the alternative. Acquiescing to fear might seem easier. But the cost of living less than the life God intended is also steeper than it appears.

I still get hurt, but I am learning to love my glass half-full. Whenever I'm tempted to go back to the way I was, I return to the One who drank the cup that looked half-empty one dark night.

Jesus. He fills my cup every time.

If you try to hang on to your life, you will lose it. But if you give up your life for my sake, you will save it.

Luke 9:24 NLT

extending our god watch

~jen schmidt

I watch. I wait. I wonder. Some call it courage. Some call it foolishness. I call it faith.

"Honey, I'm not quite sure what the Lord is trying to teach us, but we've been through this before and He's proven faithful. We will make it through again. Are you up for the adventure?"

Six months ago, I invited friends to join our family as we entered another "God Watch" period in our life: my husband's unemployment. Years ago, I coined that phrase for our children as a spiritual game of sorts, a continual, faith-building activity that invited our children to watch and then wait expectantly on the Lord's movement.

During difficult and challenging circumstances, our family sought out God Watch moments each day to remind us of the Lord's continued work in our lives. It helped us choose to refocus, even when we didn't want to, and now it's become a family mantra.

Our God Watch is a reminder to gaze at His goodness and to rest in His reassurances, but more importantly, it's a whisper of willingness to choose joy in the midst of doubt. It has cemented who I am and where my worth is found, but it doesn't come without its challenges. This unknown is extremely difficult. With a simplistic faith, I am convinced God is faithful and wants His best for my family, but admittedly, I never assumed I'd need to revisit this invitation.

Ten years ago we went through a devastating business loss. We learned all those necessary lessons then, didn't we? Why is He having us go through this again?

People assure me that everything occurs in God's perfect timing, but it's hard to reconcile that with my timing. Yet here I am, six months into our God Watch.

These months are painful and raw. With five children and a depleted emergency fund, this is a story that I didn't know would need to be rewritten, yet every page turned whispers God's grace in miraculous ways.

You see, Satan would love nothing more than for subtle seeds of doubt to creep into the crevices of my heart. *The mortgage is due. The car needs a new transmission.* He's attempting. *"Sorry, honey, they aren't hiring. I don't have an interview."* He's waging war and his desire is for disbelief and discontent to take root and permeate to the core. *"Mom, can I go on the youth group retreat? No? Why not?"*

Today, I have a choice. Yes, just today. I am taking things day by day.

God's faithfulness reminds me that I have no other choice than to punctuate my life with praise.

Praise for His security during times of uncertainty. Praise for this time of growth, hard lessons, and even unearthing my own selfishness. Praise for the little things, which are often the big things, like the way the stars twinkle so much brighter when I'm snuggled atop the trampoline with my husband and kids, or the way our eldest teenage son guzzles the soda straight from the two-liter bottle as I type.

Today, I'm not even annoyed. I am just grateful he's journeying through this difficult time with us and gifting us with his choice to be "an atypical teen" during this learning transition. He's leading his siblings well by being a strategic part of our family unit and I'm so thankful.

And I have praise for my latest God Watch moment. My favorite grocery store is tripling their coupons and three of my favorite items are on sale and yes, I have coupons for them.

Finding such joy in these seemingly insignificant things deepens my faith walk, whereas before I often missed them. This time is not about me, even though so often I make it just that. This time is about my Savior slowly chiseling away to reveal more of Himself.

Yes, this extended God Watch season is growing me deeper, making our family more intentional, and revealing to us the little blessings that are so often overlooked.

Contentment. It's here. In the midst of my deepest uncertainty, He is meeting me so personally and He is meeting our family's every need. Not our wants, but our needs. Needs are good.

So here's to month seven and the continued journey.[1]

I invite you to join me on your own God Watch as we wait expectantly, watch fervently, and wonder with anticipation at all the Lord has in store during this adventure.

> Continue in prayer, and watch in the same with thanksgiving.
>
> Colossians 4:2

---

1. This season of unemployment lasted thirteen months, and the family's God Watch moments continue.

lessons learned

I realized that the deepest spiritual lessons are not learned by His letting us have our way in the end, but by His making us wait, bearing with us in love and patience until we are able to honestly to pray what He taught His disciples to pray: Thy will be done.

Elisabeth Elliot, *Passion and Purity*

where feet may fail

melanie shankle

I've just felt overwhelmed for the last month or so. There were a few days in early January when I thought to myself, *Well, I have officially begun my descent into full-blown agoraphobia* because I didn't really want to leave my house and I certainly didn't want to think about speaking events I'd already committed to do, or whether or not I'd commit to more. Because here's the secret that I'll share: I feel so inadequate. Off the top of my head I can think of at least 4,052 people who are better than me.

That's what kept running through my mind. *I can't do this. I can't balance my time between work and family. I have no wisdom to share. I'm not enough. I'm not good enough, I'm not smart enough, and doggone it, I don't even know if people like me.* Stuart Smalley was a dad gum liar.

But then about a week ago I was driving to meet some friends for lunch and secretly maybe wishing I'd get the flu so

I would have an excuse to continue to be a social recluse (I'm envisioning all of you now second-guessing your assumptions that we'd be friends in real life because now you're overcome with the realization that I'm so weird and introverted) when Hillsong United's song "Oceans" came on.

As I listened—really listened—to the words, I felt God say to me, *You feel like this is too much because you're trying to figure out how to do it on your own power and none of this is about you.* It took everything in me not to just pull the car over and cry because that's exactly it. I'm trying to be graceful and compassionate and kind and wise and discerning and loving, but I'm putting myself in charge of the production of all those attributes. And then my selfishness and pride and insecurity all rise to the top instead and I freak out because I know how lacking I am in basically every category, and then I just want to sit on my couch and watch old episodes of *Friday Night Lights* because that feels safe.

Because here's the thing: it's easier to sit on your couch than to risk failing. It's easier to sit on your couch than to be out in the world where you're vulnerable and open to being hurt or disappointed. But you know what happens around you while you sit on your couch playing Candy Crush and watching Tami Taylor? Life. Beautiful, gorgeous, fragile, heartbreaking, mind-blowing life. God has a script written for each and every one of us, no matter who we are or what we've done or how much we feel completely ill-equipped for the adventure.

We are all climbing our own versions of Mount Everest and have no idea if our oxygen will last or if an avalanche will come, but God does. And we should never underestimate the grace and the strength He will give us for whatever challenges we face. He has called us to things higher and deeper than anything we could ever hope to achieve on our own.

It's too much. It's too much for us to do in our strength because we will mess it up, but He knows that and uses us anyway. Because it's never about creating or doing or being something that's perfect. It's not about having all the right answers. It's about being His. It's knowing that He who has called us is faithful.

Since early January I've had Colossians 1:17 written on the chalkboard in our kitchen: "He is before all things and in him all things hold together" (NIV). It's weird how that never once suggests I'm the one who's supposed to hold everything together. He's holding it all. He is before it all. He uses the sinners and the weak and the things that this world views as broken and hopeless. In Him all those things come together in ways we never dreamed possible and make something beautiful where we once looked and saw nothing.

> The sacrifices of God are a broken spirit,
> A broken and a contrite heart—
> These, O God, You will not despise.
> Psalm 51:17 NKJV

it can't just be about the blog post

deidra riggs

Yesterday's sermon had me squirming in the pew, so I drove out to the local vineyard after church. (It's not what you think.) I didn't even change my clothes. I just grabbed my camera, my phone, my laptop, my Bible, my pen, my purse, my keys, and my bottled water and jumped in the car.

I was missing the point.

Yesterday's sermon was about abiding in Jesus, and our pastor talked about the part in the Bible where Jesus says He's the vine and we are the branches. Then we walked through the part in the Bible where Jesus says that if we haven't been abiding in Him, it doesn't matter if we do good things and stay out of trouble and tell people how much God loves them. Without Jesus at the root of it all, we're just blowing hot air and it is all pointless.

Whatever I do that doesn't have its root in Jesus? Well, it may look good and sound pretty and make people feel special, but it will have no lasting impact. And what good is temporary?

When I got home from church after hearing that message, I needed a word picture. I needed to know what it looked like to abide in Jesus, because I don't want to do temporary. That's when I remembered the vineyard, packed up all my technology, and started driving. Clearly, I reasoned, God wanted me to abide at the vineyard and He would meet me there and share deep insights with me, and I should record them right away to report back to you on Facebook and Twitter and Instagram. Immediately.

At the vineyard, I got the Wi-Fi password from the guy at the front desk, opened my laptop, and readied my iPhone for photos that I could instantly share in my Twitter stream so that you wouldn't miss out on anything. But there was no connection. No matter how I tried, I could not get connected to the internet, and my iPhone refused to take any photos. In retrospect, I am quite sure God must have been shaking His holy head.

So there I sat. Totally disconnected. And that, I think, was the point.

Sitting there at the vineyard, I leaned back in the white plastic chair and gazed up at the sky. Slowly, I packed up all my technology and put it back in the trunk of my car. Then with my camera in one hand and the hem of my maxi dress in the other, I wandered the pathways that wound through rows upon rows of grapevines.

I leaned in between the leaves and stared at the small, pink grapes forming on fragile stems. Sunlight warmed my

121

shoulders and my sandals pressed down in the soil. I got up close and saw that the vine is rugged and strong. The gnarled and twisted vine made me cry and I took a step back, even though I wanted to reach out and touch it. I could see small branches being grafted in and trained to stay close to the vine. And I kept asking, "What are you saying, God? What's next?"

I noticed tendrils that reached for the sun—away from the vine. They were beautiful. And fruitless.

I know what God says about being fruitless and I gazed at one of those beautiful, wayward tendrils and said, "I wonder what's going to happen to you?" The answer was at my feet, where dry, brown, fruitless tendrils that had been cut from the vine lay. Dead.

Seeing those dead, wayward branches on the ground at my feet while birds sang concertos and the breeze ran its fingers through my hair and the sun beamed brightly overhead in a spectacular sky? It was heavy. "What are you saying, God? What's next?" I asked.

Stay close.

If God speaks in words, I think it's a whisper. It's not that booming voice Charlton Heston heard.

It was the whisper that got through to me. It was that whisper that made me realize there probably isn't anything more important than staying close to God. Not my family. Not my paycheck. Not my health. Not this blog post. Not any blog post.

When I go off searching for God just so that I'll have something to write about, I think I must be a bit like that wayward tendril that looks really good with its green leaf against the

turquoise of a Nebraska sky on a Sunday afternoon. It might
be beautiful, but it's fruitless.

I don't want fruitless.

God, I don't want fruitless.

> You did not choose Me, but I chose you and appointed
> you that you should go and bear fruit, and that your
> fruit should remain, that whatever you ask the Father
> in My name He may give you.
>
> John 15:16 NKJV

jesus and the barefooted man

elizabeth w. marshall

In the sixties she sat on red velvet and stared at dead
    mink eyes
Staring back at her while she listened to the sermon
Teased hair, hats and some white gloves, confetti
    sprinkled among the faithful
The South, the Methodists,
The pearls, sprinkled on a few
Folks listening or planning lunch at the Country
    Club later
Prime rib or fried chicken, thousand island or blue
    cheese, sweet tea or sweet tea

And now she wonders about the man with no shoes

The one my husband told me about, that day he went
    to the Episcopal church
Without me
I cocked my head and tried to get a visual on the
    thought

We walked to church together, my husband and I, a
    few Sundays later
Down a tree-lined street, dripping with moss
On more than a few old oaks
Passed him, smiling big, he not us
You're going the wrong way aren't you?
Headed away from church
The barefooted man, not us
Yeah, going to teach Sunday school
Cheshire cat grin on the barefooted man

And that was the man with no shoes
Seen through the eyes of the lady who wears the
    pearls, sometimes
And we sat and rocked and smacked some jaws and
    asked some questions
Later with folks on the porch
Because this is our sometime home
Who was that man in the bare feet
We asked

And there were opinions and there were things said
And it is still the South
And that is good not bad, but true
Really, we all have a story
And this was an old Episcopal church, after all

Suits and ties, after all

The more I thought
And wondered and took myself down to the deep
    soul places
I had to dream and cry out to myself
Come Lord Jesus and teach us

Now, how to love all the barefooted souls
Who sit among the mink and pearls

Show us how to love like you
And smile like we are all barefoot
Walking in the wrong direction

Heck, I think every man Jesus touched
Back in the dusty sandal days was barefooted
Walking

I want to walk beside
And wash and love

All the feet
And know the name of the barefooted man

I loathe labels
But I do love a Cheshire cat grin on a barefooted man
    running after Jesus
In the "wrong" direction.

How beautiful are the feet of them that preach the gospel of peace, and bring glad tidings of good things!

Romans 10:15

when you think it's about blogging, and then it's not

shelly miller

The place between comfortable chatter and quiet holiness is a doorway without hinges for acceptance. I walked through it at a blogging conference.

Carrying inspired words from platforms at this conference, I traded the beauty of the masses for a prayer room of candlelight, hushed voices, and women silently dancing like marionettes around 453 journals, writing words of encouragement. And suddenly I was captivated by the possibilities hovering over deep brokenness seated around the room.

Sinking into a high-back armchair like a child seated at an adult feast, her tiny frame bends over her knees in an arc, hair hanging down like shiny black curtains framing her face. I notice the repetitive movement of her frail hand cupped with wads of tissue toward her face, sopping up surrender.

Glancing up intermittently from her central place in the room, she offers a tilted smile of kindness to sympathetic sojourners brushing past her knees. And I see myself in her countenance.

Drifting in a boat of solitude longer than seems adequate, I recognize the expression of isolation on a stranger's face now like the jawline of my kin. Instead of looking past the uncomfortable pool of sadness, I'm drawn to it, like a lamb startled by the voice of her shepherd and running to him.

I feel the pain of isolation's process, like shadowing a terminal illness and living to tell about it. Recharged by what death's bony clutch intended to suffocate, I am a purveyor of hope's breath.

Bending over, I touch her knee gently and whisper, "Would you like me to pray with you?"

Her watery eyes look straight up, into mine, and she whispers in response, "Yes, I would, that would be nice," while pressing the ball of tissue under her nose. We collect our notes, books, and purses and move to an out-of-the-way place in the room, huddle together, and talk.

As we hold hands, she pours out the ache of lonely struggle and I have a revelation. I realize that while rocking in my empty boat on the uncertain waters of this season of life, my obsession with weather reports was misplaced. I was attempting to harness outcomes before they took place and all the while God was pushing the oars through deep water, moving us closer to shorelines crowded with brokenness.

I couldn't see above the waterline of my circumstances because I was supposed to trust where He was leading instead of trying to figure it out.

I was concerned about lightning strikes to my steel boat, asking Him why I was trapped by undesirable and unwanted situations, and I was missing the point. He was preparing me to deliver a hopeful message. The pain of isolation is the schoolroom for empathy to do her work.

Life—it's not about what you think. It's not about the perfect outfit, your beautiful business card, or how many people "like" you. It's not about platforms, microphones, your bank account, or marketing campaigns. No, those are all distractions, aren't they? Because life, your life, is about relationship with Jesus. It all goes back to how much He loves you—for you, not for what you do.

Your story of survival while alone in a tiny boat glugging with difficult circumstances is a life raft for those who are perishing without hope.

Don't you want to know the secret to finding your true self, your purpose, and your calling? This is it: give yourself away with abandon and don't waste a minute (see Matt. 16:25).

I don't want to set up kingdoms for myself. I want to deliver His kingdom through the doorway without hinges, to those longing for purpose and meaning, those who struggle to find it. That's what I learned at this conference. (And we thought it was about blogging, didn't we?)

This is my commandment, That ye love one another, as I have loved you.

John 15:12

the generous, very kind gift

robin dance

It was the best of times, it was the worst of times, it was the age of wisdom, it was the age of foolishness, it was the epoch of belief, it was the epoch of incredulity, it was the season of Light, it was the season of Darkness, it was the spring of hope, it was the winter of despair, we had everything before us, we had nothing before us, we were all going direct to heaven, we were all going direct the other way—in short, the period was so far like the present period, that some of its noisiest authorities insisted on its being received, for good or for evil, in the superlative degree of comparison only.

Charles Dickens, *A Tale of Two Cities*

I hear his words but barely; they're traveling through fog, mud, weary ears. *"Mom, there's a rainbow in our front yard."*

I am working on a deadline; my laptop is growing from my fingers. I'm perched on a barstool in our kitchen, my favorite writing spot in our home because it's the heart of where we live. Our front yard is behind me and I'm facing the back. If I bothered to look over the counter I'd see our shiny but ever-smudgy oven, then our kitchen table, and out the large picture window an ivy waterfall spilling over a red-brick wall, and then grass and trees and eventually a fence that hides our neighbors. It's storming outside.

It's storming inside too.

This has not been a good day, the kind that makes my eyes leaky faucets. Intermittent tears flow, sometimes for good reason and sometimes just for spite. I feel crazy.

I wonder if it's my age. The upper side of mid-forties has been Dickensian—

Best. Worst. Wisdom. Foolishness. Belief. Incredulity. Light. Darkness. Everything. Nothing. Despair. Hope. Heaven. The other way.

Life's journey encapsulated in a few words, brilliant, succinct, and in perfect cadence. I wish I could write like that.

This day has brought the kind of news that hurts; not death or disease, nothing as serious as that, but the little blows that bully and bruise the heart.

The rain ministers to me, a persistent, percussive splatter. Thunder captures my soul's expression . . . furious, brooding, dark, and intense, but soon it will pass.

I'm lost in more than thoughts and words when he repeats himself, louder and insistent, *"Mom! There's a rainbow in our front yard!"*

My despair is a heavy shroud, but the edge in his voice cuts through the haze and compels me to turn around and look.

I'm stunned. There's a tiny rainbow in our yard, thirty feet from our front door. I look to my right and see its end melting into the place where forest meets grass; I look to the left and it disappears into the opposite forest. I imagine that's where the gold lives.

I didn't even know baby rainbows existed!

I felt like it was Christmas morning when I was seven—wide-eyed, giddy, overwhelmed with goodness. I grabbed my camera just in time to capture two images before the rainbow faded from view.

Tears filled my eyes, *a g a i n*, but for a different reason this time, because I *knew*—

This was *my* rainbow. *A gift.* A generous, very kind gift from God.

I almost missed it, this miracle in our front yard. But I'm convinced God was patiently waiting for me to see it, *to enjoy it* with someone who would delight in it as much as me, someone else who would *see* the miracle. The Divine. *The gift.*

At the very moment I felt forgotten and unworthy, God showed me otherwise.

I am known and loved.

Soli Deo Gloria.

And when it rains on your parade, look up rather than down. Without the rain, there would be no rainbow.

G. K. Chesterton (attributed)

able

annie f. downs

$\mathcal{I}$ needed to hear from Him. If you know me, you know I would probably rather make a joke or listen to your story than admit I am living a story that confuses me.

I reached a point this week where, even though I wasn't pursuing it wholeheartedly, I knew what I needed most was a word from God. I wanted to hear Him, and at the same time, I didn't. *I feel confused enough today*, I thought, *I don't need to add attempting to hear God in these complicated situations.* (By the way, this is messed-up thinking. Don't agree with me. I came around. Just keep reading.) So I sulked. So I sat in my own confusion and wondered if I was capable of doing all the things that were on my plate. Work stuff, boy stuff, future stuff, weight stuff. So. Much. Stuff.

I drove my car to a local coffee shop called Frothy Monkey, my mind spinning. By the time I pulled into the driveway, I knew for sure—I wasn't capable. It was too much. My friend

Ashley was just leaving and she approached my car. She pulled something tiny out of her pocket and placed it in my hand. She said, "Annie, I just wanted you to have this. I prayed and felt like this was for you."

I looked down, and in my palm was a stone heart engraved with the word *ABLE*. I turned it over and over, massaging every rough spot of stone, actively trying to control my tears.

Even when my heart was too stressed, too worried, too nervous to listen to Him, He spoke. Clearly. Reminding me that I was able. That nothing He puts before me is ever more than I can handle (with Him right beside me, of course). That I am always on His mind.

My plate isn't less full. I haven't figured out any of the stuff previously listed. But I have this heart to remind me—I am able.

And so are you.

> [He] is able to do exceeding abundantly above all that we ask or think, according to the power that worketh in us.
>
> Ephesians 3:20

letting your dirty feet rub against the dirty feet of your neighbor

maggie whitley

We were gathered around in a circle playing games: a vibrant mix of little boys and girls from the Compassion program—dressed in their best clothes—along with a few program directors and our team.

The beautiful African children were showing off their favorite games and the songs they loved to sing. There was one leader in particular who I couldn't stop watching. She was wearing a purple satin floor-length dress with a heavier, darker blanket wrapped around her tiny waist. Her hair was woven into teeny tiny braids then pulled back into a ponytail. Her voice was loud and confident as she spoke to the kids;

even though she spoke in Swahili and I couldn't translate her words, I could understand her love.

At one point this leader separated the boys from the girls and they stood facing each other in a half-circle. She picked one child from each side, gave them both a small stick to hold, and told them to run around the opposite gender group—whoever made a complete circle first, won. The kids played a few rounds and it seemed simple.

Super, super simple.

Then the leader asked two people from our team to race. If you know how to predict scenarios, you'll know to put me down for the GIRLS team. She yelled something and I knew that was our cue to start the race. So off I went, running to the edge of the boys' half-circle and then behind them, quickly running across to the other side.

I could hear everyone cheering for us. *Go Maggie! Go Maggie! Go Scott!*

I could feel my adrenaline building—I needed my legs to keep up with my brain. I could feel them starting to buckle as I turned the last corner to run home, and my heart was pounding and the kids were cheering for us. Their smiles were so bright they were practically glowing, lighting up the humid, sunny day a little bit brighter. (Come to Tanzania if you don't believe me, *wink!*) I was so close to finishing first, to beating my teammate.

But I totally hit the dirt. I could blame it on the fact that my feet were sweaty inside my shoes and my legs were moving faster than my brain was spitting out commands, but I know that's not true.

137

I hit the dirt because God wanted to show me something. I remember writing yesterday that God has been trying to teach me that my earthly struggles don't matter. He wants my purpose to be stitched up by Him. And yup, He's still mending me. Earlier today He added another stitch to my heart.

Back to the race—I was about to hit the dirt, and then I did fall—it happened so fast I hardly had time to process it, but when I stood up and saw the damage, it was pretty hard to miss the dirt covering my arms and shirt and pants, and I felt a teeny bit embarrassed. There I was, our day at the child development center had JUST begun, and I was covered in dirt.

Everyone was so sweet—asking if I was ok and telling me how close to the finish line I was—telling me how great of a job I did. A few came over and patted me on the back, Zack gave me a little wink to silently remind me it was ok that I just fell. (Thanks, babe.)

My feelings had time to settle just a bit, but only just long enough to turn into a fierce embarrassment over how dirty I was.

That's when my heart broke. I could feel my eyes starting to burn, a few tears filling up each eye. I turned around for just a second and acted like I was brushing the dirt off my pants. *Oh, my arms are filthy too. I better brush the dirt off my arms too while I cry with my back to the rest of the group.* But after those few seconds passed, the tears didn't stop. Actually, the burning in my eyes increased and those few tears turned into too many tears to count. But God was

counting.

One of the little girls came over to check on me. She couldn't have been more than four years old. She saw my tears and moved a little bit closer to me. Then another girl came over and started brushing the dirt off my pants. A third came over and did the same to my shirt.

How can it be that at the start of a second I'm standing here in Africa, feeling so incredibly embarrassed that I fell—my once-clean outfit is now covered in dirt—and at the end of that one second I'm feeling the love of Christ like I never have before?

These children didn't care about my clothes. They didn't care that my now-dirty clothes looked just like their always-dirty clothes. Why couldn't I see that before? We didn't speak the same language but my tears spoke to them even more quickly than they could fall onto my cheeks. They saw me hurting and they rushed to my side.

Earlier this year, when I agreed to travel with Compassion, I had absolutely no clue about the lessons I'd be learning. I thought I was agreeing to travel to teach lessons. *Geez, how selfish does that sound?* Oh, it was so hard not to bring all of these children home with me. I mean, aside from how beautiful and spunky they are, they have so much to teach us . . . like how life is so not about how clean your clothes are or what your house looks like or whether you have to share a car with someone else in your family.

Life is about loving on each other—all the time—in the name of Jesus. "*The King will reply, 'Truly I tell you, whatever you did for one of the least of these brothers and sisters of mine, you did for me*" (Matt. 25:40 NIV).

Life is about letting your feet rub against the dirty feet of your neighbor and feeling like you know your purpose. Because we all have a purpose *and it is beautiful.*

Whosoever therefore shall humble himself as this little child, the same is greatest in the kingdom of heaven.

Matthew 18:4

hope and encouragement

Be of good courage, and he shall strengthen your heart, all ye that hope in the Lord.

Psalm 31:24

hold together

shannon lowe

The Son is the image of the invisible God, the firstborn over all creation. For in him all things were created: things in heaven and on earth, visible and invisible, whether thrones or powers or rulers or authorities; all things have been created through him and for him. He is before all things, and in him all things hold together. And he is the head of the body, the church; he is the beginning and the firstborn from among the dead, so that in everything he might have the supremacy. For God was pleased to have all his fullness dwell in him, and through him to reconcile to himself all things, whether things on earth or things in heaven, by making peace through his blood, shed on the cross.

Colossians 1:15–20 NIV

We recite those verses in our church every Sunday morning. It's a hefty theological treatise about who Christ is, with lots of nice, churchy words scattered throughout.

But did you see that little phrase tucked in verse 17? Every Sunday morning I read it and sigh a very deep sigh: *and in Him all things hold together.*

All things hold together. *Yes.* They do.

I'm sure a scholar of Scripture could expound on the theology of that verse for you in ways I cannot. Maybe "all things hold together" is speaking on the cosmic level, or the molecular one, about Christ's place as holder-together of the very fabric of the universe.

But it isn't *theology* I'm thinking when one of my children comes home from school brokenhearted or another pours my moisturizer on the bed. Or my friend's husband leaves. Or one son tells me he hates his brother, or the dog throws up on the carpet. Or I feel like I'm standing at the outskirts of my own sanity, ready to walk away. Or Hubs is late for dinner or the garage door won't open or another young soldier dies in the desert. Or I've blown it, big-time, bigger than ever before, and I'm not sure where to go from here.

In Him all things hold together.

When I'm holding on by a thread, or not even holding on at all, in Him there's rhyme for the reason and footing on the slipperiest slope. I can't tell you how, or why, but it's right there in my heart—*right there* where all the pieces feel ready to fly apart.

Where things are spinning.

Where they hurt. Right there at the very core of it all, something—*Someone*—holds me together and gently whispers the things a Father says.

Yes, He holds together the cosmos and the church and the vast arc of human history, but He also holds together the heart of His messed-up child.

No wonder I sigh.

> For we are saved by hope.
>
> Romans 8:24

good intentions

tina anderson

I love going to the store early in the morning because there are usually no lines and it's clean and quiet, with plenty of good parking spaces. Early shoppers know how to grocery shop. They understand and adhere to aisle etiquette. They know what they are doing. They are my people.

But this is not about grocery store etiquette. This is about how good intentions wear off around 9:00 a.m.

On a recent early morning shopping trip, I passed through the bakery area where I saw a mom-type person reach into the doughnut case, snag one with the tissue paper, and scarf it down in about two bites. I do not judge her, because who among us has not been overcome with doughnut fumes and passed out in the self-serve case? She had probably gotten out of bed an hour before with the best of intentions to make it a better day, to do better, to treat her body like the temple that it is.

But by 9:30, the morning sun had scorched her good intentions. Resolve dissolved. I get that.

Two aisles before I even got to the photo department, I heard a voice—intense and purposeful and rising like a thermometer. When I turned the corner I saw a harried mom with four kids hanging off the cart. She was trying to work the self-service photo print machine and her four kids were trying to work her last nerve. And then she lost it. She bellowed at the source of her exasperation and melted down into a puddle of what appeared to be good intentions.

She had probably gone to bed the night before promising herself that today would be a better day, that today she would do better; today she would be the kind of calm and reasonable mom parenting books promise you can be.

As I headed toward the checkout, I met up with a man with sad eyes and a red, bulbous drinker's nose. He wore a defeated expression. He bowed awkwardly and kindly waved me into the line ahead of him, although I had several things in my cart whereas he only had a case of beer.

"Thank you so much, sir," I said. I looked into his eyes and what I saw was the cruelest kind of sad—self-disappointment. Had he gotten up a couple of hours earlier with the best intentions to make it a better day, to do better? Yet here he was buying a case of beer at 9:30 in the morning.

Beer is not my thing, but sometimes it's the doughnut. Or the promise not to yell or be snippy and short with people I love. Or any number of shortcomings from a long list.

Like those people, I wake up each morning telling myself that today I'll make it a better day; today I'll do better. And then the sun rises in the sky.

The early shoppers, the ones with the good grocery store etiquette and a cartful of busted best intentions, they are my people.

Daily, my good intentions fail, but His compassions for me don't. And therein lies my hope.

> Because of the LORD's great love we are not
>   consumed,
>   for his compassions never fail.
> They are new every morning;
>   great is your faithfulness.
>   Lamentations 3:22–23 NIV

when it seems like it's just one trouble after the next

jennifer dukes lee

The rain wouldn't stop. It fell in thundering sheets, pooling in farm fields and backyards. Water ponded in basements, sneaking in while the world slumbered. This is the way of storms: the sky can stand calm above you one hour and then scream with rage the next. Yes, skies and mortals weep.

"Jennifer," my husband called up the basement stairs. "You'll need to come down here." I could hear the sadness in his voice. At the bottom of the steps, he held out a soggy cardboard box labeled "Jennifer's childhood memories." I had meant for years to put that stuff in plastic bins, but hadn't gotten around to it. I closed my eyes, and let my air out in one long exhale. The storm was indifferent to what I held dear, and the water had soaked straight through the cardboard.

Through tears, I pulled forty years of memories out of the box, laying it all before a whirring fan, praying I could save most of it. My baptism certificate. My high school diploma. The first news story I ever wrote, at age fifteen. My baby book. First tooth. First snip of hair. Every school photograph, kindergarten through senior year.

I cried with the sky, cried over all of my wet stuff. And yes, it was just stuff. It will be stained, is all. Storm-stained but not destroyed.

Above us and around us—and sometimes even inside of us—thunderheads are building. Out of nowhere, it seems, storms spill from the torn fabric of an iron-gray sky. Or maybe from behind the closed doors of the doctor's office, or on the other end of the phone line, or right at your own front door. I spent many years as a news reporter. I covered some of the most horrific events imaginable, proving true the Bible verse that begins like this: "In this world you will have trouble" (John 16:33 NIV). *Will*. Not might. Will.

Reading those words, you might be inclined to keep your doors locked, your phone off the hook. You might avoid getting too close to someone who wants to love you, because you never know when the storm will come, sweeping away your joy in a torrent. Except that there's more to that Bible verse. That verse doesn't end in trouble. *It ends in power.*

Jesus then said this: "But take heart! I have overcome the world." The day after the storm seeped into our basement, staining a box full of memories, the creeks bulged and raged. And a few miles away from our front door, a teenage boy fell into Beaver Creek. The boy's friends went for help and found a man named John Lems, a retired firefighter.

Later, John told local TV news reporters that he thought about throwing that boy a rope. But if the boy grabbed for the rope, he would have had to let go of the tree that was keeping him from going under fifteen feet of rushing water.

Today, the old news reporter in me called John to find out the rest of the story. John told me that he knew the boy was scared and the river was awfully cold, but he could see that the boy was strong. And he would need to just hang on. John said this: "I yelled out to the boy, 'Yes, it's cold! But I'm not going to throw you a rope! You're going to be all right *if you just hang on to that tree!*'" And so that boy hung on to the tree. And he kept hanging on until the rescuers arrived.

When trouble comes—and trouble *will* come—when the river through your life swells and rages; or when the creek

bed cracks dry; when the storm marches across the sky, or maybe straight across your heart; you will be scared. And it might feel cold. You might be tempted to grab for a sorry substitute, begging for the false hope of a rope.

But friend, you are strong. *Hang on to the tree that is even stronger.* Hold tight to the tree that has already redeemed you, the tree that bore every ache you could fathom, the tree onto which every sin was nailed. Hold on to the tree that held your Savior.

And you and I? We can be each other's Jonathan, like John Lems shouting from the shore, a reminder that "You're going to be all right *if you just hang on to that tree."* There's nothing on earth that can uproot that tree or snap the Savior's promise for you. *Don't let go. You've already been rescued.* The world and all its storms have already been overcome. And when the storm passes by, you'll find that the Calvary tree held firm. You might be storm-stained and scarred and a bit broken, but look to the sky. For you'll see it above you—the heaving dark will have given way, at last, to the sun.

And you'll know, for sure, that the light has won.

He calms the storm,
So that its waves are still.
Psalm 107:29 NKJV

mask and cape

angela nazworth

As soon as the blue mask slides down his forehead and covers three-quarters of his face, my son disappears and before me stands Batman. Batman eats my son's food, cuddles with my son's favorite blanket, and plays with my son's sister. But he will not answer when my son's name is called. Or if he does respond, it is only to remind me that he is Batman.

I play along. But he doesn't fool me. He's my boy. It takes just one moment for me to pick him out in a crowd. I know every single cowlick of his tousled blond head. I know when his aquamarine eyes hold mischief, delight, or a mixture of each. I know his laugh, his gait, and his voice (even when it is disguised).

He can call himself Batman. He can fight bad guys and save damsels like Batman. He can stand erect with his hands on his hips and his cape floating around him, but still, he doesn't fool me. I know him. He's mine.

Truth be told, he knows he isn't tricking me. After all, he doesn't dress up to pull the wool over my eyes. He dresses up to play a role. He dresses up because when you're three, it is fun to pretend that you are someone else. Someone heroic. Someone strong. It's also healthy.

And when you are slightly (mild throat clearing inserted here) more than three decades old, it is sometimes fun to pretend that you're someone else too. Someone who is strong . . . invincible even. Someone who can solve unsolvable problems. Someone who owns a heart immune to chipping . . . freezing . . . rusting . . .

But when you are a grown-up, it is not healthy to assume a whole new identity. It is not good for the soul to hide away from reality. It is a sign of insecurity and not strength to mask weakness and not answer to your own name.

Yet still, I do it. I pretend that I am capable of handling anything that comes my way . . . all by my little self. And sometimes I get so wrapped up into the role I inhabit that I do not even respond to my own name when it's whispered by Him. It's almost comical, because I know I'm not fooling God. And honestly, I'm not trying to fool Him. I'm trying to fool myself . . . trying to hide away from truths about myself that can be painful to accept . . . painful to examine . . . painful to change.

But even when I hide, my Father knows me. He calls me. He helps me untie my cape and remove my mask. He forgives me. He encourages me. He loves me.

I am His.

> Everyone on the earth should believe that he has something to give to the world which cannot otherwise be given.
>
> G. K. Chesterton, *Robert Browning*

outward aging, inward renewal

dawn camp

I always intended to age gracefully. I still feel twenty-five on the inside, so I imagined my outside would accordingly reflect that. Boy, was I wrong.

My body—which managed to birth eight babies and maintain my high-school weight—has lately turned traitor, and the number on the scale has begun to creep higher. My eyes have changed dramatically in the last year and require fancy and expensive contact lenses for me to both read and see distances (less clear than before) at the same time. The face in the mirror often looks older, more tired than I'd like. Some days I just want to yell, "Nobody told me this was going to happen! I didn't sign up for this!"

So much for aging gracefully.

Recently I heard a sermon on 2 Corinthians 4:16, how our bodies age but the inward man renews daily, and something inside of me clicked: God doesn't look at the wrinkles at the corner of my eyes. He doesn't look at my waistline or the number on the scales. God looks at my inward man—the part He put there and whose job it is to reflect and glorify Him— that He renews daily.

I look around me and see women whose bodies have aged but whose lives serve Him by example and by the wisdom they share with others. That inward part of them that loves the Lord and that He loves in return is unworn, unwrinkled, ageless. Their service may be less physical, but they serve nonetheless.

This perspective has transformed my thinking radically and I am encouraged: God can use me at any age and in any stage.

> But though our outward man perish, yet the inward man is renewed day by day.
>
> 2 Corinthians 4:16

courage

leeana tankersley

Life shrinks or expands in proportion to one's courage.
Anais Nin, *The Diary of Anais Nin*, vol. 3

On Monday night I spoke at a women's event at my church, which was such a sweet homecoming for me. I talked about courage, and what it means—to me—to be a person of courage.

Courage comes from the Latin word *cor*, meaning "heart." I believe we all want to be people of the heart. We don't want to be marking time, living in survival mode, eking life out. We want to be flourishing, living from a very awake and alive heart. We want to live from the broad grace, the expanse, the spacious place.

This requires courage. Mainly because many of us carry chaos inside us that is unresolved. This chaos creates a level of

discomfort, dis-ease. When we hit up against the raw places inside us, we have a choice: numb or respond.

It takes courage to respond. It takes courage to feel. It takes courage to put our phones down and look up at the world. It takes courage to get up off the couch. *It takes courage to make one small step in the right direction.*

We get stymied because we assume acts of courage are sweeping declarations or 180-degree resolutions when, I believe, courage is really about taking the very next step in front of us. When we take that next right step, our one part of courage is met with a thousand parts of God's grace. And we can make a long journey that way. One little step at a time.

I've seen this truth in my own life. Transformation happens in small steps of courage. One after the other.

Is there a next step in your life that God's been nudging you to consider? Seeing a doctor. Going to a meeting. Calling that friend. Acknowledging a desire. Surrendering a dream. Taking a prayer walk. Meeting with a counselor. Signing up for a group. Could you, in an act of courage, turn toward that next step today?

We come into contact with our own discomfort. We respond by taking one small step. We believe (even in our unbelief) that our small step of courage will be met with God's limitless grace. And we find that we can make a long journey one incremental step at a time.

I believe in you.

> Courage is not simply one of the virtues, but the form of every virtue at the testing point.
>
> C. S. Lewis, *The Screwtape Letters*

hope

shannon lowe

My hands dug at the ground tentatively. It had been some time since I'd been able to think beyond my next breath, and productivity felt foreign. But there I was, on my knees, in a flower bed in my backyard, breathing the chilly November air and thinking of spring.

It was late autumn and I was emerging, ever so slowly, from the darkest time of my life. For months I had been paralyzed by depression and anxiety. But as November arrived and the earth began to fall asleep for the winter, something inside me began to awaken. Medication, prayer, and the love of my family had pulled me back from the brink, and I stepped out of my "bunker," blinking in the sunlight and walking very slowly. *But I was walking.* Gently forward, each day a little easier than the next, I was moving toward Hope.

And so it was I sat in my flower bed that day, overcome by the need to get my hands in the dirt. I had some hyacinth bulbs that had been tucked in my fridge for some time, and I knew I needed to get them in the ground before the first freeze. I turned the bulbs over in my dirty hands—they looked like misshapen onions, with brittle flakes coming off the sides and dead-looking scraggles sticking out of the tops. I stared at them for some time, marveling that something beautiful would shoot out of that clumpy brown mess in just a few short months. But with faith in my soil and my Miracle-Gro, I tucked a few bulbs into the ground.

I sat back and patted the ground where they were buried. They were powerful symbols to me of my own journey—something ugly and dead-ish, held in the hands of a Creator who wasn't afraid to get His hands dirty.

My bulbs lay still and waited for spring. My heart waited with them.

And spring indeed came, both to the hyacinths and to me. In an explosion of electric blue color, those gorgeous bulbs gave me their very best that March. And I, further down my path of healing, was able to rejoice—in the beauty of a blue flower, in the warmth of spring, in the faithfulness of a God whose mercies are new again and again.

Those dark days are now a distant memory and my steps are no longer slow and tentative. Sometimes it's easy to forget just how dark those times were. But then every year spring comes, and every year those plucky hyacinths show their faces to me, reminding me of my long journey toward hope. They appeared this weekend, and I greeted my old friends (though not for long, as they were mowed down by an unforgiving GI Joe truck).

I laughed, and I remembered, and I gratefully turned my face to the sun.

In him was life; and the life was the light of men.

John 1:4

worship

Wherefore we receiving a kingdom which cannot be moved, let us have grace, whereby we may serve God acceptably with reverence and godly fear: For our God is a consuming fire.

Hebrews 12:28–29

i saw you, jesus

jennifer dukes lee

I saw You, Jesus. You were in the back pew, with Your sad eyes and Your two boys who wouldn't sit still. Their dad was home, asleep on the couch.

I saw You. You were in the corner of the conference-room hall. You were praying that someone might save a spot for you at a table. You were in the diaper aisle, Jesus, with twenty items on your grocery list but only enough money to pay for twelve.

I saw you, Jesus—but sometimes? I walk right past You. You are the scruffy-bearded guy with the cardboard sign on the street corner. You are the overworked executive who hasn't seen his family in a week. You live in Haiti, and You live down the street. I have Your unanswered email in my inbox.

You are the beggar, the lonely, the overlooked, the weary mother, the desperate, the out-of-style, the head-hanging-low. You know where the hidden bottles are, and how to make a life go numb. You know where the pills are, in case You want to call the whole thing off. I saw You, Jesus. But did I serve You? Or did I simply look over Your shoulder?

Lord, I beg You. Make me a servant. Cause me to sit in Your pew, to kneel down in the mess on Your kitchen floor, to hold Your dirty hand in mine. Because I wonder: Have we gotten too big for our britches, that we can no longer serve You in the ditches? You are right in front of us.

How do we keep overlooking You? You're in our newsfeeds and our living rooms, but are we looking over Your shoulder for something, or someone, we find more tantalizing to feed our hungry hearts?

Dear God, make me a servant.

Jesus, You put off the privilege of heaven for the grit of earth. You gave up the throne room for the basin. You were the only one in the history of forever who was worthy to be served, but this is what You did instead: You put on an apron. You knelt. You washed feet. This, You said, is how You would show the full extent of Your love.

You had more titles than a Nobel Prize–winner, but always pointed to the Father. You wowed people with miracles, then told them to keep quiet. You fed thousands, then stole away for quiet moments alone, away from the limelight. You weren't about celebrity; You were about serving.

Lord, I want to serve You, just like You served. I want to serve You, but how often have I missed You sitting in the corners, the classrooms, the cubicles, and the carpool lines? How often have I chased glitter? Lord, I beg You: break any platform, microphone, blog post, or book of mine, if it does not bring glory to You alone. We were not made for fame or fortune but for the Father. Strip me of any desire in my crowded heart to be known or applauded. Don't let me get paralyzed by popularity or praise.

Make me a servant. Don't allow me to overlook the overlooked. Take me to dark corners. Make my hands dirty. Break my two-faced heart. Give me an apron and a basin. Because Lord Jesus . . . I don't want to get to heaven and find out that, despite all I ever said or wrote or preached or tweeted, I had missed out on the chance to serve You. To kneel beside.

To wash the feet of a King.

> But by love serve one another.
> Galatians 5:13

he sees you

joy forney

Today, I want to encourage you to be God's *you*. And what if you feel like you work hard and no one notices? You pour out your heart, your time, your life, and you are not seeing the results that you want? You feel like no one sees you? Well, I want to introduce you to a friend . . .

She goes by Tinang Kule, which simply means, "mother of Kule." Her real name? I don't know . . . I have never heard it. It, like her personal identity, has been quieted . . . never to be spoken again. Her life is given in total sacrifice to others; even her own name is sacrificed and she is known only as the mother of her firstborn. Her day begins early. She starts the fire to begin cooking so that others might eat. It is hot and laborious work.

She smiles and sweats. She is happy that everyone likes her cooking. The satisfied nods of appreciation are enough for her. She stokes the fire and carries on.

Task runs into task as she continues to cook and clean, care for and nurture. She hears the MAF—Mission Aviation Fellowship—airplane overhead and she rushes to get a brown paper–wrapped package full of fried rice for the pilot . . . *my husband*. She is intent on having it there for him when he arrives. Each day she does this, for whichever pilot might land in her village to serve her people.

She rushes down the dirt road with a thermos full of hot tea and the brown paper package. I am humbled. She asks me if I have any laundry. I sheepishly say yes. She picks up the bag of dirty clothes and we walk to the river. She crouches down and begins to beat the clothes one by one against a rock, a rhythm of beating and twisting and soaking and twisting again. I try to help . . . The kids bathing nearby in the river giggle as I, the white lady, try to do it right. It is difficult and monotonous.

I whisper to the mother of Kule, "This is so much work . . . It doesn't matter, you don't need to wash our clothes."

She replies with a big smile, "Oh no, I love to wash clothes."

And she means it. Seriously? She loves to wake up early when the only thing to look forward to is serving? Where is her recognition, her moment in the spotlight? Where is her *identity*? She doesn't even have a name to call her own. Tears spring to my eyes. Am I willing to do the same? To go unnoticed? The answer, embarrassingly, is no. NO.

Sure I am willing to sacrifice, to serve my family, to go mostly without recognition. But there is that little part that wants to be known, to be recognized, to be called by my name.

She smiles and I see Jesus all over her. His is the name that she is known by . . . it is her identity. He sees her. And it is enough. It is E-N-O-U-G-H.

He sees *you*. He is proud of *you*. He adores *you*. His praise is the only praise we need. His love fills our need for *identity*.

He will quiet you with His love,
He will rejoice over you with singing.
Zephaniah 3:17 NKJV

labor of love

sarah markley

We had lice in our house yesterday. It's really something I don't like to talk about, even here among friends. It is so much easier to keep this private because *you* don't want to be the reason the whole school issues a "disease" warning, and if you are, you don't want anyone else to know it's *your* kid. But you don't keep quiet. You call the school and tell everyone you know that we-are-staying-home-today-to-pick-out-lice.

People think you are dirty or not clean or something (even though you are very clean) and they make assumptions (still) about hygiene when someone gets lice. It's almost like you are a pariah and your home is a source of disease for even the people who love you the most. But it's what happens when you have school-aged girls with long, untamed hair that is hard to catch in a hair tie for more than a few hours.

So we scrubbed and picked and lice-shampooed. We combed and sprayed and tore apart the house and everything soft and fluffy went into the washing machine in the hottest water. We swept and vacuumed and changed every linen in the entire house. I opened all the windows and doors. *Fresh air, please come in.*

I sat for three hours, two different times, bent over the head of a girl-child, using my fingers through long, deep hair, scouring them clean. I can only call it an intimate labor of love. There are very few people you can call to come search your scalp for insects, as very few people will even enter your house when the L-word is used.

But nonetheless my back is almost broken today because yesterday I bowed it to make sure these children's heads were fixed and mended.

My eleven-year-old, with her thick, auburn hair, sat patiently as I silently combed. I was in the middle of my second hour on her head. She said something softly. "Thank you, Mama. I don't know anyone else who would do this."

"I love you, sweetie," I said as I adjusted the towel over her shoulders. "It's what I do."

And it's familiar, this child sitting close to you; nearly an embrace, but it's not. It's a cleansing.

I only wonder if this is what Jesus does with us. He pulls us close, not worrying if the dirty will rub off on himself, and gets to work on the mending.

This cleansing of us is dirty work. There are parts of it that shouldn't even be spoken of in good company. It's the picking and scrubbing and the death and the need. The intense need! This is something that one cannot do alone. We need someone else to do this washing for us. *But it's also intimate.* It's close and humiliating to have someone else look at the ugly, dirty parts of you. It's embarrassing to have someone else know that you need this so deeply and to be still held close during it.

When the girls had gone to bed late last night, after the last nit comb had been sterilized, I pulled a chair under the light. "Chad, it's my turn now," I said to my husband. And I bent my head for him to look and touch my scalp, behind my ears, the top of my head. For an hour we remained like this, his body close to mine in this intimate cleansing.

It is a labor of intimacy that only love can perform.

In Christian service the branches that bear the most fruit hang the lowest.

Author Unknown

in the season of rain, pray for rain

lisa-jo baker

I pray at the kitchen sink more than anywhere else. I think it's something to do with the soothing warm water and the fact that washing dishes is a focused task. Compared to, say, cleaning up the living room, which has me rabbit-trailing between toys and books and the old carpet stain I keep meaning to re-treat and the nagging reminder from an overstuffed basket that I need to sort through the mail. At the kitchen sink there are only dishes and soapsuds and my thoughts.

Late at night, while the household sleeps, I straggle into the kitchen between cleaning up and bedtime to find peace in a sink full of waiting dishes. *And before I know it I am turning over more than cups*; I am sharing what I find in the back of my mind with the God who meets me in my unconventional kitchen.

So as I rinse my bright red frying pan I find myself praying desperate dreams for the future. *I pray for what I want, but rarely for what I have.* Until recently I was reminded of this verse:

> Ask rain from the LORD
> in the season of the spring rain,
> from the LORD who makes the storm clouds,
> and he will give them showers of rain.
> Zechariah 10:1 ESV

In the season of rain, pray for rain. And suddenly it's New Year's Eve 1999, and I'm back on a dry game farm in Zimbabwe surrounded by farmers who haven't seen decent rain in months. These sun-weathered men sit in their rough clothes at a long table that's been set for dinner under the Southern Cross. The soft linens and delicate place settings are a quirky contrast to those seated before them ready to toast in the new millennium.

The first course is cucumber soup. But with the first bites come cold, hard drops. The soup ricochets up at those dipping spoons down into it. Rough faces and beards are splattered green. Cucumber soup everywhere but in our mouths.

Rain. Long looked-for rain pelts down from the clouds that are our only ceiling tonight. I prepare to make a dash for it—to shelter and warmth and the inside of the lodge.

But I am the only one to move. A table of grown men carries on their meal as the rain falls down and the soup splashes

175

up. The thunder and force of the water is so loud that it crowds out any attempt at conversation. But their actions speak louder than words and my father interprets them for me, "They won't leave the rain because they don't want it to leave them." In the season of rain, they want more rain. And they are afraid if they get up it will be over.

With soapsuds up to my elbows I lean on the sink, remembering. *What I have now is what I once wanted so desperately*: healed marriage, healthy children, incredibly meaningful work. I don't want to lose sight of these in the chase after my next prayer request.

In the season of rain—still—pray for rain. *Presume nothing; take nothing for granted; treasure everything.* Because once the rain begins and sends soup splashing all over you, it's tempting to walk away from the answered prayer and move on to the next thing.

I do not want to do that. I want to sit and revel in what God has given me here and now. I want it to splash up and onto and all over me. I want to pray for its protection and its continuation.

Daily, between soapsuds and dirty dishes, I want to pray for what I have.

The Lord will open to you His good treasure, the heavens, to give the rain to your land in its season, and to bless all the work of your hand.

Deuteronomy 28:12 NKJV

prayer like tweeting

seth haines

My phone lit up over the lunch hour yesterday, the Twitter messenger notification popping up again and again. It was a friend, the writer sort who spins sentences about as well as anyone this side of the Mississippi. I had asked her if she planned on writing a book in the near future, and she was working her explanation out in bite-size messages typed with two thumbs.

"ALL THE NOISE," she typed in an all-capped exclamation, and I knew what she meant—*so many books, so little time, so much marketing.*

An email cut through the direct message conversation. It was another friend asking about a recent trip I had taken to Ethiopia, and he was trying to pin me down, trying to peg a date, time, and location so that we could catch up. Before I could respond, a Facebook notification distracted me, informed me that I had been tagged in a post, and as I was reading said post, my wife, Amber, texted me to ask about some item of family business.

Ping. Buzz. Blip. Ding.

We live in an age of uninterrupted interruptions. Divided between here and there, at any given moment we ship parts of ourselves to friends in Texas, others in the UK, and the spouse across town. Yesterday I was at lunch with all of these people, virtually anyway, and I felt drawn and quartered, divided among too many good people.

I wonder whether the human species is evolving yet again, whether we are sitting under some technological personality fission—*homo discidium*, we are becoming. I wonder whether our DNA is undergoing a culling, the human capacity for singular presence being stripped from its code.

This morning I sat in my chair, trying to find the rhythm of meditation. Instead, I found myself in popcorn prayer with God, a thousand thought-kernels expanding all at once. It was a distracted, divided prayer with no staying power—*be with my kids today; and what about that project that's due? And when do I lead worship next at church? I think Amber has yoga tonight*—and so on and so forth. The divided me has learned to pray like a social media interaction. Quick. Bite-size. Throwaway.

This morning, though, I stopped, took a breath, and centered on an old orthodox prayer a Catholic priest once taught me. In rhythm with my breathing, I prayed, "Lord Jesus Christ, son of God, have mercy on me, a sinner."

And then I waited.

In the silence of the heart God speaks. If you face God in prayer and silence, God will speak to you.

Mother Teresa, *In the Heart of the World*

music moments

laura boggess

This morning I iron his shirt and press a neat crease in his black pants. His dad ties his tie and we declare him handsome. He gathers his music and I drive him to the middle school, where he kisses my cheek and leaves me.

Break a leg, I whisper, as that long yellow bus pulls away from the curb. His face grows smaller in the window and I just watch them go. He'll be making music with his classmates all day—playing for judges who will rate their performance. They've practiced weeks for this—his teacher hired a special percussion tutor to work with him and his mates.

"Are you nervous?" I had asked, as we sat in the parking lot waiting.

"No, not really," he said, shrugging it off. "We've been practicing a lot."

I looked into his young face and saw that it was true. He was right there with me in that moment. Not worrying about the next. Still, we prayed together and I kissed my drummer-boy gone. His leaving left me empty.

Why do I? I wondered, all alone in the car. Why do I let things of this world make me nervous—make me worry—when I've prepared so hard? Is my practicing all in vain? I drive home in the cold and my heart feels frozen.

Later I sit with coffee and my Bible unopened in front of me. I watch a downy woodpecker tap at the frozen suet in the feeder. He clings to the pole with his four toes—two in front, two in back—and hammers incessantly at the stubborn block. "I know how you feel," I murmur.

With a sigh I open my Bible—taking a random plunge, desperate for a word. It's Matthew 6:28. *And why do you worry about clothes?* my NIV asks. *See how the flowers of the field grow.*

I like my NIV—the New International Version—it's been a good friend. The pages are dog-eared and the margins scribbled all over. But my spirit wants the old words—the words I grew up hearing in the King James Version of the Bible. So I rummage around and find it. And I find these words: *And why take ye thought for raiment? Consider the lilies of the field, how they grow; they toil not, neither do they spin.*

I stop here because, as a living Word does, it is speaking a new thing to me.

Thought for raiment. Isn't this what I do? Don't I dress myself in my thoughts, let planning and learning and all that is in my head cover me? Too often, I take thought for raiment—not only do I worry about what I dress myself in, but *I dress myself in that worry.*

181

Consider the lilies. I leave both Bibles open and rise from the table. I've had my Word. I move to the window and study the meadow. There is a flash of red that burns against the white of the snow-covered forsythia—Mr. Cardinal waiting a turn to feed. All the lilies of this field sleep beneath frozen soil, but his carmine presence speaks grace over their slumber.

When did I get too busy to see the way the white frocking laces in and out of leaf and grass—woven with an expert hand? The way the elbow of the tree cups the snow with such tender care it makes my bruised heart ache for such a branchy embrace. The meadow is dressed for a wedding and I almost missed my invitation.

Mr. Cardinal is joined by his bride and they crown this silvery gown—two blushing, beaked lilies, preening just for me.

Worry does not empty tomorrow of its sorrow, it empties today of its strength.

Corrie ten Boom, *Clippings from My Notebook*

and so we are carried along

amanda williams

Two years ago, I stood in line at the neighborhood grocery checkout counter with a box of cake mix, cupcake liners, snacks, streamers, and two number 1 candles. I was exhausted in every way—soul weary from clinging hard to faith, heart weary from clinging hard to hope, body weary from wearing thin the road from home to the hospital and back again.

My babies and their sister were at home, and there I was mama as best as I could be. My mother and father were at the hospital, and there I was daughter as best I could be. There my mother and brother and I locked arms through our first six-week crash course in ICU—the protocol, the etiquette, the vocabulary, and the ever-awakeness of the place. It was our first grueling lesson in how to stare death in the face, the death of one we love. How to be pressed so closely up against it that the pain of loss began to set in. How to look upon it

183

unflinching while keeping a fist gripped fast on life. These were the weeks we first discovered the blurred line between the two, between death and life. Where we found first the ache and agony, the beauty and glory distinct to that indescribable threshold, that holding place where we were forced to stay too long. And yet we did not want to leave. Leaving might mean crossing over.

I stood in that checkout line with makings for a last-minute party for these unexpected baby boy blessings, and I was part present but mostly away. My heart had staked its ground in those other places and that is where I stayed.

The items were grouped on the grocery counter according to the orange vouchers in the yellow folder—dairy in one group, produce in another, birthday trappings and the rest in a third group at the back. I handed the yellow folder with the vouchers to Edward the cashier, and he marked down totals with his pencil. I'd gone over on the produce again and so I apologized. Why could I never seem to get that part right? "It's ok," he explained. He could add the overage to my other items and I could pay for it all together. I gave a weak, appreciative smile and let my eyes travel back out the window.

Why did I feel so self-conscious of those orange vouchers even now, a full year in? I only brought out the folder when feeling especially brave; most days I scanned the lists with it tucked out of sight in my bag. Our friends and family knew— to them I sang WIC's praises, unashamed—but strangers and acquaintances were a different matter. It felt too personal, too tender. Oh, the formula costs must be outrageous, friends would say, and nod with understanding. But the truth is we were relieved when it paid for the milk and cheese too.

The last year had been wrought with blessing and struggle. We'd lost two houses, gained two babies, and quit one job in a few turns of the calendar, and we were fighting to make payments on this life we'd built together. This beautiful, chaotic, full life in this beautiful, creaky, old house—we loved it, every ounce. We trusted all would be well, and for now trusting meant taking what we wished we didn't need.

The items were all scanned and Edward repeated the total, and I swiped the blue card through the machine. "Swipe it again," he asked, and so I did. He looked up and gave a sympathetic half-smile, and I knew the charge hadn't gone through.

It wasn't the first time. *But today, of all days?* I looked in my wallet knowing full well nothing was there and then back up to his eyes. And that is when the tears came. Tears came often in that year, what with the hormones and the hospital and the joy mixed in thick, but I could hide them when I needed to (like in line at the grocery store). But this time they came full to my throat and eyes and I had no heart-muscle left to keep them in. I mumbled something to Edward and the bagger between sobs about my boys and the birthday and the family at home waiting, and I could see my dad lying in that hospital bed, not dead but not yet fully alive, and I saw every fear and failure of my motherhood and daughterhood and wifehood there in that shopping cart of food I could not afford, and I wept. In front of God and Edward and everybody, I wept like a child.

Edward said he could suspend the transaction and so I said, "Yes, please." Except that produce on the voucher? That would have to be paid for and the rest voided out, and so he did. Item by item, he scanned them again until only the bananas and vegetables were left. I owed $1.97 now, he said, but I didn't have it. And before the tears could begin a second run, Edward whispered "I've got it," and pulled the cash out from his pocket and put it into the register. I offered thank yous and I'm sorrys to his refrain of "It's no big deal, it's just two dollars." It was not just two dollars to me.

I went home and hugged my husband and cried, knowing how this would make him feel, knowing how hard he was working to make his one income into two, knowing how his worth and our bank account are inextricably linked in his gut even though his head and his heart know and believe the Truth. I stayed behind with my girl and one-year-old boys as he drove back to the store and looked Edward in the eye and handed over two dollars and said thank you. And I was no less proud to be his wife then than I am now when he deposits a paycheck into our account or pays the mortgage of our century-old house.

And that is how our first couple years as a family of five looked. Exhaustion, gratitude, hospital visits, sleeplessness, fear, joy, uncertainty, and provision. We were carried by our neighbors and our friends and our family and strangers and Edward the cashier. We were carried by government-supplied baby formula and home-cooked meals made by loving hands and delivered to our door. We were carried by nurses and doctors who cared for us inside hospital walls and prayed for us outside them. We were carried by the One whose cattle cover a thousand hills, who created and sustains us, who knows our going out and our lying down.

   This One, He carried us then and carries us still but some days, many days, I forget. I believe the lie that it all rests square on my shoulders and I nurture quiet pride that I hold it up so high and so well. I forget the unseen Hand that delivers life from death and food to lips. But that day at the grocery store I could not forget. That day, and so many since, I am made to remember.

   And so I thank God for those days in the checkout line when the account had all but run dry and we drew from the Well with water full. I thank God for the yellow folder that, even now that it's gone, reminds from whence my true help comes. I thank God for you, stranger, and for you, brother and sister, and for you my friend at the playground who catches my boys before they run out the gate and into the street. I thank God for you, for through you He has carried us and He carries us still.

Bear ye one another's burdens, and so fulfil the law of Christ.

Galatians 6:2

this do in remembrance of me

dawn camp

Saturday evening services, annual meeting, and somehow I've forgotten it's communion until I walk into the sanctuary: men and boys on one side, women and girls on the other. This is my seven-year-old daughter's third time to take part; I tap her on the shoulder from behind and she beams, sitting with her friend.

I take a seat beside a church sister who's alone too. She welcomes me and whispers that we've never taken communion together, smiling.

We sing a capella, sweet harmonies, old minor hymns. The children request a faster, lighter song, but it's not what I want to hear. The final song is called, and I nod and breathe deep.

> Just one more time before the door
> Of death would intervene
> They gathered there to sup and share
> Love's feast in joy serene.

For Christ aspired, strongly desired
To meet in fellowship here
With those who talked with Him and walked
Along each dusty year.

He gave them bread and wine so red
And told them when they meet
"Remember Me when this you see,"
Then knelt and washed their feet.

When next we meet in mem'ry sweet
Let love and fellowship flow
For this might be the last for me
Before I onward go.
"The Last Supper," *Old School Hymnal*

Past, present, future, it's all here; I remember members of my family who have gone on and envision future generations sitting in these pews, tears in their eyes, singing the same songs.

Our pastor talks about the communion bread, symbolic of Christ's body, broken for us, and how the Jews thoroughly swept the leaven (yeast), which represented sin, from their homes before the Passover. The tray passes to me and I slowly grind the unleavened bread between my teeth.

The congregation sits still, silent, thoughtful, and I feel the Holy Spirit is among us here. Then comes the wine, a symbol of Christ's blood, shed for the sins of his people. I drink and feel the warmth in my throat.

These first two parts of the service involve the vertical relationship between us and God. This last part is horizontal, fellowship among us here. I take a towel and kneel on the floor, pulling a basin of water from beneath the pew in front of me, and then I lift my sister's feet, one at a time, washing them in the cool water as my rings softly scrape the metal pan. After both feet are wrapped in the towel and patted dry, we smile and embrace, and then she kneels to wash mine.

We talk softly about my mother and how we both miss her, and of her father-in-law, an accomplished gardener who for years made the communion wine himself before he passed on. Tears gather and we smile again, and I know similar hushed conversations are taking place throughout the room. We rise and embrace our brothers and sisters: spirits refreshed, wounds healed as we do this in remembrance of Him.

It's good to be in the house of the Lord on this night.

> And he took bread, and gave thanks, and brake it, and gave unto them, saying, This is my body which is given for you: this do in remembrance of me.
>
> Luke 22:19

contributors

Kayla Aimee is a mama to a toddler so she spends her days covered in peanut butter and grace. She lives in the South with her husband and daughter, where she enjoys scrapbooking, storytelling, and sweet tea. She writes about faith, family, and her favorite things at www.kaylaaimee.com.

Tina Anderson is an artist, photographer, and writer. She writes about the joys and challenges of late-in-life motherhood and other random things at *Antique Mommy*, where life is sometimes sweet, sometimes tart, but always real; www. antiquemommy.com.

Lisa-Jo Baker is the author of *Surprised by Motherhood: Everything I Never Expected about Being a Mom*. Her writings on motherhood are syndicated from New Zealand to New York and you can catch up with her daily chaos at LisaJoBaker.com.

Laura Boggess writes from a little valley in West Virginia where she lives with her husband and two sons. When she's not blogging at lauraboggess.com, you'll find her at thehigh calling.org. Her latest book, *Playdates with God*, released in the fall of 2014.

Stephanie Bryant is the cofounder of incourage.me. She is a new mama to Gabrielle and the Creative Mastermind at www.sbryant.me. She's a courageous God-sized dreamer, lid lifter, and visionary schemer. Stephanie is always excited for the next God-sized adventure.

Dawn Camp is a photographer, wife, and mother of eight who lives life with a camera in one hand and a glass of sweet tea in the other. She lives in Atlanta and blogs about family, faith, and Photoshop at MyHomeSweetHomeOnline.net and at incourage.me.

Mary Carver is a writer, church planter, wife, and mom. She's also a recovering perfectionist who loves YA novels, way too much television, and eating M&Ms by the handful. Mary writes about her imperfect life with humor and honesty at www.givinguponperfect.com.

Married to her college sweetheart and mom to three, **Robin Dance** longs for Neverland and Narnia. She's as southern as sugar-shocked tea, laughs freely, and believes in the power of hugs. Don't miss her poignant memoir and lifestyle blog, robindance.me.

Mary DeMuth is an author and speaker who loves to help people live uncaged, freedom-infused lives. She's written sixteen books, her latest being *Not Marked: Finding Hope and Healing after Sexual Abuse*. She lives in Texas with her family. Find out more at marydemuth.com.

Christin Ditchfield is an author, conference speaker, and syndicated radio host, and is passionate about calling women to a deeper life—the kind of life we long for, the life we were created for! She blogs at www.WhatWomenShouldKnow.org.

Annie F. Downs is an author, blogger, and speaker based in Nashville, Tennessee. An author of three books, *Let's All Be Brave*, *Perfectly Unique*, and *Speak Love*, Annie also loves traveling around the country speaking to young women, college students, and adults. Read more at anniedowns.com.

Margaret Feinberg is a popular speaker and the author of *Wonderstruck* and *Scouting the Divine*. Named one of fifty women most shaping culture and the church today by *Christianity Today*, she lives in Colorado with her husband, Leif, and superpup, Hershey, and blogs at www.margaret feinberg.com.

Joy Forney is the wife of a missionary pilot and mama to five. Living abroad brings her to the foot of the cross time and time again, and no matter her geographical location, she still finds Him faithful. She blogs about her adventure of a life at joyforney.org.

Sara Frankl (Gitz) entered into the arms of Jesus on September 24, 2011, but her legacy of choosing joy lives on. Her blog, www.gitzengirl.blogspot.com, is about her commitment to being intentional about embracing the story God had for her.

Emily P. Freeman is a writer and a listener who creates space for souls to breathe. She is the author of three books, including her most recent release, *A Million Little Ways*. Emily lives in North Carolina with her husband, John, and their three children.

Holley Gerth is a bestselling author of several books, a life coach, and a speaker. She also cofounded the website incourage.me and blogs at www.holleygerth.com.

Bonnie Gray is the author of *Finding Spiritual Whitespace* and the soulful writer behind FaithBarista.com, serving up shots of faith for everyday life. Her writing is syndicated on Crosswalk.com and featured on DaySpring's (in)courage. Bonnie lives in Northern California with her husband, Eric, and their two sons.

Amber Haines has four sons, a guitar-playing husband, her blog theRunaMuck.com, and rare friends. She loves the funky, the narrative, and the dirty South. She finds community among the broken.

Seth Haines is a working stiff who makes his home in the Ozark mountains. He and his wife, Amber Haines, have four boys and a dog named Lucy. Seth enjoys music, food, fly-fishing, and fine sentences. You can find him on a regular basis at sethhaines.com.

Jennifer Dukes Lee is a grace dweller and storyteller at www.JenniferDukesLee.com. She and her husband live on the family farm in Iowa with their two girls. Jennifer is the author of *Love Idol: Letting Go of Your Need for Approval—and Seeing Yourself through God's Eyes.*

Kelley J. Leigh is a midlife writer and mom to four sons. Kelley lives in a quirky little mountain town in Colorado where she writes openly about intimacy issues and recovery in marriage and faith. Find her over at www.kelleyjleigh.com.

Lisa Leonard creates jewelry out of her California workshop. She and her husband have two sons, one with special needs. Their story of finding beauty in brokenness is woven through every product they create and through her blog, LisaLeonard. com.

Shannon Lowe blogged for many years at www.rocksinmydryer. typepad.com. Her writing has appeared in numerous books and magazines, including *Good Housekeeping*, *Parenting*, and *Chicken Soup for the New Mom's Soul.* She lives in Oklahoma with her husband and four kids.

Sarah Markley has been writing all her life but has been blogging for the last seven years at sarahmarkley.com. She's a freelance writer and speaker, and spends her spare time working for nonprofits. She loves her kids, her husband, extravagant grace, and listening to your story.

Elizabeth W. Marshall is a curious *noticer* who lives by the sea. She processes her life and her world by painting with words. Elizabeth and her family live in a small shrimping village where she is content to go exploring by bike, by boat, or by foot, recording her journey and gathering inspiration along the way. Her poetry and prose appear on her writing home/blog wynnegraceappears.com. She is happiest when her three children and her husband (and their dogs) are gathered together for a meal.

Shelly Miller is an author and speaker who helps people think differently about life through storytelling and beauty. As a photographer, coach, clergy wife, and mother of teenagers, she feels most alive surrounded by diversity and culture. She blogs every week at RedemptionsBeauty.com.

Angela Nazworth is a recovering perfectionist who blogs mostly about the beauty of grace, vulnerability, and community for incourage.me and her personal blog, angelanazworth.com. She is a wife and a mother of two who manages philanthropic communications for a nonprofit, national healthcare association.

Tsh Oxenreider is the author of *Notes from a Blue Bike: The Art of Living Intentionally in a Chaotic World.* You can find her spearheading a community blog about simple living at *The Art of Simple*, or on Twitter @tsh.

Laura Parker. Having lived overseas three times, Laura's family now calls Colorado home. She and her husband lead a nonprofit organization called The Exodus Road, which fuels undercover investigations into sex trafficking. She has published a book about their journey entitled *The Exodus Road* and blogs at www.LauraParkerWrites.com.

Katie Kenny Phillips and her husband are raising their children (both biological and foster) in Atlanta, Georgia. She writes about dirt, superhero underwear, and Legos (and all the moments in between when God shows up in the midst of a messy, hilarious, beautiful, obedient life) at www.operationleapoffaith.com.

Rachel Anne Ridge is an artist and writer, mom to three grown kids, and Nana to two littles. She blogs daily humor and encouragement at www.HomeSanctuary.com. Her first book, *Flash, the Donkey*, will be released by Tyndale in May 2015.

Deidra Riggs and her husband live in Lincoln, Nebraska. They are the proud parents of two adult children and the happy inhabitants of an empty nest. Deidra is managing editor at thehighcalling.org, a monthly contributor to incourage.me, and blogs at deidrariggs.com.

As a full-time family manager, **Jen Schmidt** embraces both the beauty and bedlam of everyday life at beautyandbedlam.com. You can find her seeking truth, establishing family traditions, shopping the thrift stores, creating ten-minute dinners, or hosting the Becoming conference.

Arianne Segerman is a freelance writer, a blogger, and a mom to three crazy boys and one little girl. She loves walking the journey of life and faith through hiking the mountains of Arizona as much as she loves gushing about fashion and style. She shares about all of it with grace and beauty on her blog mabelandriv.com/blog.

Melanie Shankle lives in San Antonio, Texas, with her husband, Perry, and daughter, Caroline. She writes daily on TheBig MamaBlog.com and is the *New York Times* bestselling author of *Sparkly Green Earrings* and *The Antelope in the Living Room*.

Kristen Strong is wife to a retired Air Force veteran and mom to twin sons and a daughter. She lives in the Rocky Mountain country of Colorado and writes of the fresh-air hope found in Jesus at her blog chasingblueskies.net.

Leeana Tankersley is a writer, Navy wife, and mom to Luke, Lane, and Elle. Her newest book, *Breathing Room: Letting Go So You Can Fully Live*, is about finding space when we feel overwhelmed. Follow Leeana at www.leeanatankersley.com.

Jessica Turner is the founder of popular lifestyle blog *The Mom Creative* and author of *The Fringe Hours*. Additionally, Jessica is an (in)courage writer, World Vision blogger, and cohost of the Bloom Book Club. She and her family live in Nashville, Tennessee.

Ann Voskamp is wife to the Farmer, mama to six, and the *New York Times* bestselling author of *One Thousand Gifts: A Dare to Live Fully Right Where You Are* and *The Greatest Gift: Unwrapping the Full Love Story of Christmas*. She blogs wild grace at aholyexperience.com.

Edie Wadsworth is a momma, writer, blogger, foodie, cowboy boot wearer, and hospitality fiend. She's a lover of truth, beauty, and goodness, and seeks to inspire women in their love and service of others at the lifestyle blog www.lifeingraceblog.com.

Kristen Welch is a blogger (wearethatfamily.com) and the author of *Rhinestone Jesus: Saying Yes to God When Sparkly*

Safe Faith Is No Longer Enough (Tyndale 2014). In 2010 she and her family founded a nonprofit, Mercy House Kenya, that empowers pregnant mothers living in extreme poverty with opportunity. Between writing and saying yes to God, Kristen enjoys life in Texas with her best friend and three awesome kids.

Maggie Whitley is a lifestyle blogger and handmade shop owner (Caroline-made and The Gussy Club) living in Los Angeles with her husband, son, and pup. Maggie began sewing in 2008 and has been blessed with many challenging adventures, all which have brought more glory to God than she could ever have imagined.

Lisa Whittle is an author, speaker, ministry leader, wife, and mother. With her honest and bottom-line approach, Lisa speaks Jesus, shares stories, and starts conversations. Her passions include eclectic things, art, truthful conversations, and words that heal. She loves one man, three kids, one dog, and above all, The Great One. Connect with Lisa at www.lisawhittle.com.

Amanda Williams is a writer in love with honest words and the way they make us feel less alone. Mother to one girl and twin boys, she lives and works in a loud farmhouse outside Nashville, Tennessee. Amanda shares stories of imperfect motherhood, faith, and writing at life-edited.com.

Get to know

Dawn Camp

Read her blog

&

Join the conversation

• MyHomeSweetHomeOnline.net •

Be the First to Hear about Other New Books from REVELL!

Sign up for announcements about new and upcoming titles at

RevellBooks.com/SignUp

Don't miss out on our great reads!

a division of Baker Publishing Group
www.RevellBooks.com